JMT

JOURNAL • OF MORAL THEOLOGY

NON-HUMAN ANIMALS

Edited by John Berkman, Charles C. Camosy, and Celia Deane-Drummond

JMT

JOURNAL • OF

M • O • R • A • L

THEOLOGY

Journal of Moral Theology is a peer-reviewed scholarly journal focusing on Catholic moral theology. It is concerned with contemporary issues as well as our deeply rooted tradition of inquiry about the moral life. Our mission is to publish scholarly articles in the field of moral theology, as well as theological treatments of related topics in philosophy, economics, political philosophy, and psychology. *Journal of Moral Theology* is published semiannually, with January and June issues.

Articles published in the *Journal of Moral Theology* will undergo at least two peer reviews. Authors are asked to submit articles electronically to jmt@msmary.edu and will be informed about the review process by e-mail. Submissions should be prepared for blind review and conform to *Chicago Manual of Style*. Microsoft Word format preferred. Editors assume that submissions are not being simultaneously considered for publication in another venue.

ISSN 2166-2851 (print), ISSN 2166-2118 (online). *Journal of Moral Theology* is published by Mount St. Mary's University, 16300 Old Emmitsburg Road, Emmitsburg, MD 21727.

Pickwick Publications, An Imprint of Wipf and Stock Publishers, 199 W. 8th Ave., Suite 3, Eugene, OR 97401. www.wipfandstock.com. ISBN 13: 978-1-4982-1909-9

Journal of Moral Theology, Vol. 3, No. 2 (2014): 1-10

Introduction

Catholic Moral Theology and the Moral Status of Non-Human Animals

John Berkman and Celia Deane-Drummond[1]

THIS ISSUE OF THE *JOURNAL OF MORAL THEOLOGY* features a collection of essays with an approach to a topic you've never read about in book or journal form. That is because there has never been a collection of academic essays entirely from the perspective of Catholic moral theology on this particular topic. And what is this topic? Morality and non-human animals. More specifically, it is about, for example, particular elephants, chimpanzees, dogs, dolphins, hyenas, pigs, cats and hominids, and also all these animals (and others) as members of a particular species not simply as objects for human moral concern, but rather, as moral subjects.[2] This collection features essays about these elephants, chimpanzees, dolphins, etc. as God's creatures worthy of being *subjects* (not merely objects) of moral concern. And it also features essays about higher non-human animals as potentially (or actually) moral agents whose intellectual and/or moral capacities are worthy of significant and sustained reflection and analysis.

It is fair to say that as recently as five years ago giving significant theological thought to non-human animals was widely dismissed if not

---

[1] We owe a special thanks to Charles Camosy who collaborated in the editorial process for this issue, but for reasons completely beyond his control was prevented from contributing to this introductory essay.

[2] While this is the first collection of academic essays entirely from the perspective of Catholic moral theology, we would be remiss not to note the two fine monographs by Catholic moral theologians, namely Deborah Jones, *The School of Compassion: A Roman Catholic Theology of Animals* (Leominster, UK: Gracewing, 2009), and Charles Camosy, *For love of animals: Christian ethics, consistent action* (Cincinnati: Franciscan, 2013). In addition, there have been a number of excellent ecumenical collections of ethical reflection on non-human animals, including Charles R. Pinches and Jay B. McDaniel ed., *Good News for Animals? Christian Approaches to Animal Well-Being* (Maryknoll: Orbis, 1993), Andrew Linzey and Dorothy Yamamoto ed., *Animals on the Agenda: Questions About Animals for Theology and Ethics* (London: SCM, 1998), Celia Deane-Drummond and David Clough ed., *Creaturely Theology: On God, Humans and Other Animals* (London: SCM, 2009), and Celia Deane-Drummond, Rebecca Artinian-Kaiser and David Clough, ed., *Animals as Religious Subjects* (London: Bloomsbury/T & T Clark, 2013).

ridiculed in the world of Catholic theology, systematic and moral theology included. Perhaps three anecdotes will illustrate the point. Only five years ago at the Catholic Theological Society of America, Elizabeth Farians, the first woman ever admitted as a member of the society (admitted with much resistance and controversy in 1965[3]) made a valiant effort to have the society devote a single yearly session in an ongoing manner to theological reflection on non-human animals. Although an interest group on non-human animals had been allowed to function for three years at the CTSA (2008-2010) and despite extensive lobbying by Dr. Farians, she was unable to generate enough interest and support to have a single concurrent session on non-animals approved beyond those three years.[4]

The second example is taken from the early academic career of John Berkman. While a pre-tenured moral theologian at The Catholic University of America in 1999, Berkman was actually ordered by his chair in the Department of Theology to cease writing on ethical issues related to non-human animals. The chair, a well-respected New Testament theologian and ethicist, ordered this because he (and presumably the department more generally) considered the very question to be unworthy of the time and effort of a moral theologian at The Catholic University of America.[5]

[3] For a discussion of the controversy over Farians's admission as a member of the CTSA, see Anne Patrick and Elizabeth Johnson, "Appendix 2: CTSA Women's Seminar in Constructive Theology: A Thumbnail History in Three Acts" in the *Proceedings of the CTSA* (2006), 218-31, http://ejournals.bc.edu/ojs/index.php/ctsa/-article/view/4845. See especially "Annex A: The Farians Incident," 223-7. One wonders if it is merely coincidental that eminent Catholic scholar Elizabeth Johnson, who co-authored the piece recounting the Farians incident, has begun to take the lives of other animals seriously, as expressed in her new book, *Asks the Beasts: Darwin and the God of Love* (London: Bloomsbury, 2014).

[4] In light of Celia Deane-Drummond's essay "Are Animals Moral? Taking Soundings through Vice, Virtue, Conscience and Imago Dei" (published in Deane-Drummond and Clough ed. *Creaturely Theology*. London: SCM, 2009), which shows analogous parallels between Thomas' treatment of the image and likeness of God in women and non-human animals, the irony of the CTSA's inability and/or unwillingness to accommodate the pleas of Dr. Farians is deep and palpable.

[5] The order came in the aftermath of Berkman's essay "Prophetically Pro-Life: John Paul II's Gospel of Life and Evangelical Concern for Animals," versions of which were published in the *Josephinum Journal of Theology* and in Linzey and Yamamoto ed. *Animals on the Agenda*. Berkman dutifully complied with the order for a number of years, but eventually decided he could not reject an opportunity to contribute "The Consumption of Animals and the Catholic Tradition," which was the "Catholic" essay in Stephen Sapontzis, ed. *Food for Thought: The Debate over Eating Meet* (New York: Prometheus Press, 2004). *Food for Thought* included 30 essays by the major "luminaries" in ethical thinking about animals, including Carol Adams, Stephen R. L. Clark, Lori Gruen, Marti Kheel, Andrew Linzey, Evelyn Pluhar, Val Plumwood, Tom Regan, Steve Sapontzis, Roger Scruton, and Peter Singer. The year "Consumption" was published, Berkman's department at CUA would turn him down for promotion and tenure, despite a publication record commensurate with promotion and tenure.

A third example comes from the academic experience of Celia Deane-Drummond, who in March 2007 presented "Animal Ethics: Where Do We Go From Here?" at a large Catholic moral theology conference. In this paper Deane-Drummond argued that Kevin Kelly's ethical methodology with regard to thinking about human embryos was relevant for consideration of non-human animals and further, that both issues deserved significant moral attention, not least because of the strikingly heated political debates surrounding both issues. However, Deane-Drummond was surprised and shocked by the comments of several of the most senior Catholic moral theologians at her presentation, who treated a serious discussion of animals as a topic of abject mirth. Rather than something to be taken seriously, animals were not part of the agenda for serious moral theologians.[6]

We could provide many more examples, but we take it that the almost complete marginalization of consideration of non-human animals in Catholic theology generally and Catholic moral theology more specifically up until very recently will be apparent to those who have worked in these fields.

But something remarkable has happened in just the past few years. No longer excluding animals from view, there is a veritable flowering of interest in non-human animals among Catholic moral theologians. Instead of accepting and reinforcing the binary between humans and animals, Catholic moral theologians now acknowledge there are "other animals" with which we share animality as common creaturely kinds, even if we note that humans are specific kinds of animals.[7] Perhaps it is that, as in other topics, moral theologians are slowly following the lead of moral philosophers, who have been writing extensively on this topic for the last forty years. But on the other hand, on related topics such as environmental ethics, Roman Catholic discussions proved to be far more open, so that elements of environmental concern

---

The Provost of The Catholic University of America would later take the highly unusual step of overturning both of the Department of Theology's decisions, promoting Berkman to Associate Professor and nullifying the department's judgment regarding Berkman's tenure.

[6] The conference was entitled, *For the Love of the Church: Essays in Celebration and Honour of Kevin Kelly*, and held at Liverpool Hope University. Fortunately, the editors of the book commemorating the conference did not share the view of these senior moral theologians, and published Deane-Drummond's paper as "Animal ethics: Where do we go from here?" in *Moral Theology for the Twenty-First Century: Essays in Celebration of Kevin Kelly*, ed. Bernard Hoose, Julie Clague and Gerard Mannion (London: Continuum, 2008),155-63. The irony of all this is that whereas Kelly's own ethical mantra advocates "graceful disagreement" where there are opposing moral views, Deane-Drummond's argues for limits to such boundaries, where some ethical views and practices are excluded as quite simply morally reprehensible.

[7] For example, following Alasdair MacIntyre, moral theologian Joseph Capizzi argues this viewpoint in "Consciousness in Human and Nonhuman Animals," *National Catholic Bioethics Quarterly* (Spring 2008), 33-42.

started to show up even in official Catholic social teaching at more or less the same time as environmental ethics was established as a field of study in the late 1960s and 1970s.[8] There is something, then, about the specific concern for non-human animals that seems to have been resisted among Catholic moral theologians. It seems that posing questions about the status of animals has been more threatening compared with environmental concerns. One possible suggestion as to why this might be the case is that, on the one hand, environmental concern, when viewed in a global context, shows the necessary relation between the flourishing of human beings and that of ecological contexts. Other-animal concern, on the other hand, seems to take away from concern for humans as it focuses on the individual lives of animals, rather than much more generalized ecological contexts for human flourishing.[9] Both ecological ethics and animal ethics challenge lifestyles in particular ways, but animal ethics arguably presses for more immediate and radical change, even among city dwellers.

Perhaps there are positive influences as well, so a shift in concern might be related to the influence of important literary works like J.M. Coetzee's *The Lives of Animals* (Princeton: Princeton University Press, 1999) and Jonathan Safran Foer's *Eating Animals* (New York: Little, Brown, and Company, 2009), or to the integration of ethical vegetarianism and veganism into mainstream restaurant and food culture. Perhaps it is the explosion of theatre releases and documentary films on the plight of domestic animals in Western culture. Or perhaps the issue is starting to be viewed more simply as an important element in the development of a more general ecological consciousness that has sprung up in moral theology since the beginning of the 21st century. Or perhaps moral theologians are starting to listen to their students, who have been declaring that animals are a moral issue in their classrooms in increasingly large numbers. Most likely it is some combination of all of these factors.

Since the past generation of Catholic moralists and theologians as a whole has ignored moral questions regarding non-human animals, Catholic ethicists interested in these questions have for the most part had to turn to Protestant theologians and philosophers for inspiration and direction. While many theologians and philosophers are worthy of discussion, this introduction will mention only three whose work either has set or should set a significant part of the agenda for future moral and theological reflection on non-human animals.

---

[8] For further discussion of this topic, see C. Deane-Drummond, "Joining in the Dance: Ecology in Roman Catholic Social Teaching," *New Blackfriars*, Vol. 93, no. 1044 (2012), 193-212.

[9] A widely publicized strain of the "animal rights" movement argued in such a way that less concern should be shown to human beings qua human beings. For more on this argument see John Berkman's "From Theological Speciesism to a Theological Ethology: Where Catholic Moral Theology Needs to Go" in this issue.

In the last forty years, the theologian most associated with engaging issues around non-human animals is Andrew Linzey, who virtually single handedly pioneered research in this field, beginning with the publication of his book *Animal Rights: A Christian Perspective* (London: SCM Press, 1976). Linzey has been a veritable John the Baptist, seeming to many to be a lone voice crying in the wilderness, with an explicit mission to wake a sleeping theological establishment, one largely immune to his arguments, as well as his pleadings and cajoling. Through books like *Animal Rites: Liturgies of Animal Care* (London: SCM Press, 1999), *Creatures of the Same God* (New York: Lantern, 2009), and edited collections *Animals and Christianity: A Book of Readings* ed. with Tom Regan (London: SCM Press, 1989) and *After Noah: Animals and the Liberation of Theology* ed. with Dan Cohn Sherbock (London: Mowbray, 1997), Linzey has become something of a household name among those who are interested in animal ethics from a Christian perspective. Among his more academic works *Animal Theology* (London: SCM Press, 1987)[10] and *Why Animal Suffering Matters: Philosophy, Theology and Practical Ethics* (New York: Oxford University Press, 2009) will be of particular interest to Catholic moral theologians. Linzey's project has not been restricted to his own academic work, as he has indefatigably encouraged scholars from all over the world to take an interest in animal ethics, most recently through the Oxford Centre for Animal Ethics. His writing has, of course, attracted great controversy, much of which we believe is undeserved and reflects a prejudicial attitude against the topic.

As for philosophers, while the utilitarian Peter Singer and deontologist Tom Regan have been highly influential in secular debates about non-human animals, their approaches have garnered surprisingly little sympathy even among those few Catholic ethicists who have taken up the subject of non-human animals.[11] A more significant interlocutor for many Catholic moral theologians—though typically on topics only marginally related to non-human animals in themselves—has been Mary Midgley, whose work has taken human (and non-human animal) bodily life very seriously in numerous works, including *Beast and Man: The Roots of Human Nature* (Ithaca: Cornell University Press,

---

[10] Linzey's *Animal Theology* was (unsurprisingly) both widely praised and criticized. Among his many critics, those from environmentalists perhaps were most unfortunate. Linzey's criticism of many forms of ecological concern because its "systems" perspective detracted from proper due attention to individual animals likely contributed to (the perhaps inevitable) parting of the ways of otherwise natural allies (i.e., animal ethicists and environmental ethicists) in the struggle against a purely anthropocentric ethics.

[11] The work of Charles Camosy is a major exception to this, having engaged Singer's work more extensively than any other Catholic moral theologian, and whose own work in moral theology and non-human animals shows the significant (though selective) influence of Singer.

1978), *Animals and Why they Matter* (Harmondsworth: Penguin, 1983), and especially her collection of essays, *The Essential Mary Midgley* (London: Routledge, 2005).

But the two most important philosophers over the last forty years in terms of the importance of their work on non-human animals for those doing Catholic moral theology have been Aristotelians and Christian philosophers. One is well-known to all Catholic moral theologians, and that is of course Alasdair MacIntyre. His *Dependent Rational Animals* (London: Duckworth, 1999) very suddenly and authoritatively gave questions about animal cognition and social life legitimacy in the circles of Catholic moral theology. Ironically, MacIntyre has published very little (so far) on non-human animals. A further irony is that MacIntyre's *Dependent Rational Animals* apparently has no interest in promoting moral concern for non-human animals: His chapters devoted to dolphin rationality and social life are merely a means to speak with insight and authority on the significance of bodily life for human beings. Nevertheless, the chapters in *Dependent Rational Animals* on dolphin life in general (and pre-linguistic cognition in dolphins and other higher animals) has without a doubt been highly significant in terms of putting non-human animals on the agenda for moral theologians.

The other Christian philosopher, whose academic work arguably surpasses that of Linzey is Stephen R. L. Clark. He is known for the range and depth of his work on an astonishingly large range of questions related to the moral significance of non-human animals. While Clark has also made very significant contributions to moral and political philosophy, philosophy of religion and environmental philosophy, he has written truly brilliantly as a philosopher and Christian about non-human animals. Whether it was his early books *The Moral Status of Animals* (Oxford: Oxford University Press, 1977/1984) and *The Nature of the Beast* (Oxford: Oxford University Press, 1982), or later books like *How to Think about the Earth* (London: Mowbray, 1993), *Biology and Christian Ethics* (Cambridge: Cambridge University Press, 2000), *The Political Animal: Biology, Ethics, and Politics* (London: Routledge, 1999), and especially *Animals and their Moral Standing* (London: Routledge, 1997), Clark has been *the* towering intellectual giant among philosophers who have been interested in non-human animals in relation to a Christian world-view. Of course, as a philosopher who has been unabashed both regarding his Christian convictions and his concern for non-human animals, one would expect him to have been marginalized in the philosophical world.[12] But for those of us

[12] Clark's work has not been entirely marginalized. His work was the inspiration and jumping-off point for the Wittgensteinian moral philosopher Cora Diamond's "Anything but Argument" in Cora Diamond, *The Realistic Spirit* (Cambridge: MIT Press, 1995). "Anything but Argument" is Diamond's 1982 essay in reply to Onona

who recognize the importance of these questions for Christianity, Stephen Clark's work is an incredibly rich resource for the upcoming generation of Catholic moral theologians who choose to devote their intellectual energies to thinking theologically about non-human animals. And both of us as editors acknowledge the key influence of Clark's work in shifting our attention to a serious study of animal ethics.

With that most brief and limited introduction to seminal figures and writings for Catholic moral theologians who wish to think theologically and ethically about non-human animals, we now turn to the contributions of the six moral theologians in this issue.

John Berkman's "From Theological Speciesism to a Theological Ethology: Where Catholic Moral Theology Needs to Go," begins with a reading of why recent Catholic moral thought has been uninterested in questions about the moral significance of non-human animals. After presenting a typology of the kinds of reasons Catholic moralists have provided for ignoring non-human animals, it goes on argue that while the *Catechism of the Catholic Church*'s brief section on the moral treatment of non-human animals is at best morally ambiguous on this topic, it provides one with enough promising elements to serve as a starting point for a renewed and developed tradition of thought within Catholicism on non-human animals. The final section of the article proposes the creation and development of a new branch of moral and systematic theology, namely a theological ethology where moral and theological reflection about the good of an individual species is brought to bear on the best of contemporary ethological studies on the affective, cognitive, moral, and perhaps even spiritual capacities of specific higher non-human animals, with the goal of moral reflection of the kinds of moral concern and/or protection due to these species in light of that reflection.

Julie Rubio's "Animals, Evil, and Family Meals" begins with a recognition of the moral significance of domestic animals who are treated cruelly in modern factory farming. While acknowledging factory farming as an evil, Rubio argues that eating or serving factory-farmed meat should be considered a potentially licit form of material cooperation with evil. Noting that the moral manuals of the nineteenth and twentieth centuries often excused material cooperation when necessary to one's vocation of providing for a family, Rubio contends that serving and cooking food is an important part of a parental vocation that can conflict with the duty to avoid factory-farmed meat. She argues that, in at least some cases, eating or serving factory-farmed meat

O'Neill's criticism of Clark's 1977 *The Moral Status of Animals*. Along with her other essays such as "Eating Meat and Eating People" (1978), "Experimenting on Animals: A Problem in Ethics" (1981), and "Injustice and Animals" (1991), Diamond's "Anything but Argument" has in turn inspired many other philosophers including Stanley Cavell, Ian Hacking, and John McDowell to engage in serious moral reflection about our treatment of non-human animals.

may be an acceptable form of material cooperation with evil. However, she contends that a commitment to grow in virtue requires increasing cooperation with good by eating and serving less meat, buying more ethically-sourced meat, and working to change social structures that make avoiding factory-farmed meat difficult.

Charles Camosy and Susan Kopp's, "The Use of Non-Human Animals in Biomedical Research: Can Moral Theology Fill the Gap?" begins with a sweeping introduction to laboratory animal use in biomedical research (BMR), including historical perspectives, regulation of BMR, and use of chimpanzees. From there, the authors present the emerging secular and moral issues around new biotechnological procedures as they are impacting animals today, including genetic manipulation for the creation of new laboratory animal strains and advanced surgical interventions in the course of experimentation. They argue that these uses of animals present new and urgent moral questions requiring theological and metaphysical concepts that secular discourse avoids. Every use or alteration of an animal in this context must respect the moral claim that the nature of that animal makes upon our behavior and on our moral duty, without reducing him or her to a mere tool or commodity. The authors propose that a moral obligation to allow animals to flourish precisely as the beings that they are can help articulate a framework for ongoing moral analysis of these technologies as they impact nonhuman animals. The article concludes with a number of suggestions for future moral reflection in this regard.

Celia Deane–Drummond's "Evolutionary Perspectives on Inter-Morality and Inter-Species Relationships Interrogated in the Light of the Rise and Fall of *Homo sapiens sapiens*" probes the classic split between human and other animals, asking less about whether humans are unique compared with other animals and more about the particular role other animals have played in evolutionary accounts of human emergence and morality. Countering the presumption that evolutionary accounts are inevitably hostile to affirming human dignity, she argues for a suitably critical engagement with evolutionary theories. Drawing on evolutionary theories of human cooperation and niche construction, she demonstrates the importance of other animal lives in the shaping of human becoming in early hominid societies, and uses case studies of hyenas and elephants to show the interweaving of human and other animal kinds through human history. More radical is her suggestion that human morality is, on this basis, an inter-morality, one that engages forms of morality found in other social animals. This presses a case further than simply attributing a form of morality to other animals and so is more sophisticated than a naïve suggestion of a linear evolutionary relationship between forms of morality in humans and those in other social animals. While she recognizes the distinctive marks of human morality, she believes it was shaped by relationships with other animals.

Jean Porter, in her "Moral Passions: A Thomistic Interpretation of Moral Emotions in Nonhuman and Human Animals," argues in favor of morality as distinctively rational, and therefore a distinctively human phenomenon. By rationality she means capacities for abstraction and self-conscious use of general concepts and inferential principles. At first sight her position might seem to reinforce the gulf between human beings and other animals that has persisted in the theological and philosophical literature. But recognizing the distinctive marks of human mental capacity is still consistent with contemporary science. Porter takes what could be termed a mediating position. On the one hand, critical of oversimplified narratives of continuity that seem to place human beings on an essential continuum with other social animals, Porter, on the other hand, also agrees with primatologist Frans de Waal that moral emotions such as sympathy and indignation are central for a human morality. Through a detailed engagement with the work of Thomas Aquinas, she argues convincingly that a Thomistic approach offers an illuminating framework for making sense of what we know about moral emotions in both humans and other kinds of animals. On this account, the passions do indeed play a central and necessary role in shaping human perceptions, volitions, and choices. At the same time she considers that such passions an inadequate basis for human morality, but nonetheless, necessary for human moral life.

James Helmer's "Speaking Theologically of Animal Rights" is an original and notable effort to explore the extent to which the language of "animal rights" can be seen as compatible with, or indeed, even logically flowing out of the understanding of human rights embodied in modern Catholic social teaching. Helmer begins by analyzing the Pontifical Council for Justice and Peace's *Compendium of the Social Doctrine of the Church* (2006)[13] and the International Theological Commission's "Communion and Stewardship: Human Persons Created in the Image of God" (2004) as points of engagement with the Catholic social tradition's understanding of moral rights, and then he puts that understanding into conversation with recent philosophical work on rights which emphasizes the "relational" character of rights. Helmer then proceeds to argue in favor of the analogous extension of moral rights to members of some non-human animal species, in virtue of their status both as moral patients (i.e., as objects of moral concern) and as moral subjects. Helmer concludes that this theological conception of the rights of non-human animals is fully consonant with the spirit of the tradition of Catholic social teaching, and can serve as an effective heuristic device for reflecting further on our various responsibilities and obligations to non-human animals.

---

13 The document can be found at: www.vatican.va/roman_curia/pontifical_councils/justpeace/documents/rc_pc_justpeace_doc_20060526_compendio-dott-soc_en.html.

In conclusion, the editors of this collection (i.e., John Berkman, Charles Camosy, and Celia Deane-Drummond) are very pleased to be editing this groundbreaking work. However, we hope that, in a way similar to the groundbreaking volumes on animals rights by philosophers and Protestant theologians, this volume will be built-on and surpassed in the very near future. As such, we invite our fellow Catholic moral theologians to both criticize and build on the work of this volume. We are convinced that a moral consideration of non-human animals is an issue of great importance, and having our work in this issue made obsolete or commented on for further critical development would be deeply satisfying.

Journal of Moral Theology, Vol. 3, No. 2 (2014): 11-34

From Theological Speciesism to a Theological Ethology: Where Catholic Moral Theology Needs to Go

John Berkman

THIS ESSAY—AND INDEED THIS ISSUE—of the *Journal of Moral Theology*—arise from a session at the January 2013 meeting of the Society of Christian Ethics (SCE) in Chicago. That year, the President of the SCE was Miguel De La Torre and the theme of the conference was to be marginalized groups and topics. This theme for the SCE inspired Charlie Camosy, Celia Deane-Drummond and I to propose a session entitled, "Ascending to the Margins: Speciesism as a Concern in Catholic Thought." We picked that title because as far as we were concerned, the issue of moral concern for non-human animals was not yet even of marginal significance for Catholic moral theology.[1]

Our goal for the 2013 SCE session was twofold: first, to show that the charge of speciesism (adequately qualified) is a legitimate critique of much of the Catholic moral tradition, and second, to argue that an appropriate response to this moral problem requires a development of Catholic doctrine and moral practice, particularly in the Western industrial context where structures of sin visit unprecedented cruelty upon untold millions of domesticated animals. The goal of this article is the same. I wish to show the extent to which the Catholic moral tradition remains speciesist, to discuss the ambivalent character of current official Catholic teaching on the moral treatment of non-human animals, and to suggest a direction towards a more adequate Catholic theology and ethics with regard to non-human animals.

This article proceeds in four parts. First, in very broad strokes I survey the scene of Catholic moral theology in the English speaking world over the last generation with regard what place it assigns to concern for non-human animals and to what extent it has been speciesist.

[1] Considering the fact that the pre-Vatican II manuals of moral theology did consider non-human animals to be a topic of moral concern, it would be more precise to say "no longer of concern for moral theology." I discuss this point at greater length in the first section of the article.

I will argue that over the last generation Catholic moral theology as a discipline failed to recognize concern for non-human animals as a topic of concern, and thus didn't even bother to assert (though latently held) a speciesist viewpoint.

Second, I present a typology of three defenses of speciesism by Catholic moralists: *zero-sum defenses*, which presume or argue that any heightened or intrinsic concern attributed to any non-human animals will necessarily or inevitably lead to a failure of adequate intrinsic concern for human beings; *rationalist defenses*, which argue that rationality (at least according to a specific way of defining it) is uniquely human and that only rational animals are worthy of intrinsic concern; and finally *abstract concern defenses*, which while notionally acknowledging that animals have intrinsic worth and deserve care and concern, in real terms fail to engage in a moral and theological discussion of the implications of this view, and thus fail to practically address the issues.

Third, I examine in detail the most significant magisterial writing on concern for non-human animals in the last generation, the 1997 *Catechism of the Catholic Church*'s four paragraphs on the subject. I say "most significant" because it is a highly authoritative and highly influential teaching of the Catholic Church, undoubtedly the most authoritative and substantial writing on non-human animals coming from the magisterium in the post-Vatican II period. It thus deserves careful scrutiny with regard to what guidance it can provide the field of Catholic moral theology. I conclude that the *Catechism* reflects the ambiguous legacy of Catholic moral theology on non-human animals, but includes resources to guide a development in Catholic doctrine and practice with regard to appropriate concern for and treatment of non-human animals.

Having reflected on the meaning of speciesism and providing an account of theological speciesism, having examined the types of defenses of speciesism, and having looked at the *Catechism's* discussion of non-human animals, in the fourth and final section I discuss some of the deconstructive and constructive work that needs to be done if a post-speciesist understanding of other animal species is to fully emerge in the Catholic moral and theological tradition. I conclude the section by proposing the discipline of theological ethology and explaining the various reasons why St. Albert the Great should be its patron saint.

Since there are many moral questions related to the treatment of non-human animals, I will focus on the question of cruelty to non-human animals. I do so because the Catholic tradition has been most clear about the wrong of animal cruelty. I also focus on cruelty to animals because it is one of the great moral evils in contemporary America, an egregious wrong being done to a variety of domesticated non-human animals on a mind-boggling scale in industrial farming in

America (and America is busily exporting that model around the world). We as leaders for the Catholic moral tradition have been conspicuously silent about it.

WHAT IS SPECIESISM?

As noted above, it is necessary to adequately qualify what is meant by "speciesism" and "theological speciesism." When Richard Ryder coined the term in 1971, "speciesism" meant the undue moral privileging of one species over another.[2] While Ryder certainly had in mind the undue privileging of the human species over all other animal species, speciesism can also refer to the undue privileging of any species over any other. For example, speciesism can be the undue privileging of dogs and cats and eagles over pigs and cows and wolves, or for that matter the undue privileging of elephants over human poachers. Acceptance of the legitimacy and usefulness of "speciesism" in itself only requires one to agree that at least some humans at some times inordinately privilege one species over another, which is obviously true.

The major objections to the very notion of speciesism as a moral term seems to have arisen by the term's association with Peter Singer's *Animal Liberation* (1975), which popularized speciesism as a moral critique. Singer's main goal in using speciesism as a moral critique was to increase human moral concern for non-human animals. Unfortunately, Singer's use of speciesism became almost inextricably linked to his variety of preference utilitarian moral theory, which refuses to attribute intrinsic goodness to any species (including human beings). On Singer's account, any creature's value depends on its ability to hold and exercise preferences ("interests" was Singer's preferred term). From this view Singer drew the logical but odious conclusion that since certain groups of human beings cannot exercise preferences (e.g., fetuses, infants, and the severely mentally disabled), they are less deserving of moral protection than (e.g., adult) members a variety of non-human species which can exercise preferences. The ironic result of the close association between speciesism and Singer's moral theory and moral views more generally was that speciesism came to be associated with reducing or eliminating the moral protection of human beings *qua* human beings, rather than heightening moral concern for non-human animals.

---

[2] See Richard Ryder, "Experiments on Animals," in Stanley Godlovitch, Roslind Godlovitch, and John Harris, ed., *Animals, Men and Morals: An Enquiry into the Maltreatment of Non-Humans* (London: Gollancz, 1971), 81. Ryder drew an analogy between racism and the undue treatment of animals. His hope was that in the same way that racial discrimination had gone from being largely condoned to almost universally reviled as "racism," so too would the mistreatment of non-humans come to be reviled as "speciesism."

In order to be adequately appropriated as a legitimate critique by moral theologians, it will be helpful to disentangle speciesism from Singer's moral theory and views and to begin by recovering its original meaning and best general definition—that by "speciesism" is meant the undue moral privileging of one species over another. Since, however, this essay focuses on the moral treatment of non-human animals by humans, the working definition of speciesism in this article is *the undue (and typically exclusive) intrinsic concern for human animals in comparison to all other animals*.

As moral theologians, our first responsibility in writing about the moral treatment of non-human animals is to understand and communicate God's story about them. That story, as I understand it, is first and foremost a story of God's providential love and concern for each species of animal, including the individuals of each species. And an aspect of God's providential love are the ends of each animal, ends by which it flourishes as a member of its species. On this understanding, part of human stewardship of our fellow creatures consists in seeking to understand the flourishing of various species and the conditions under which various species flourish. And when possible, to facilitate or at least seek to avoid diminishing the capacity of God's creatures to flourish according to their kind.[3]

In contrast, speciesism in Christian perspective (i.e., theological speciesism) involves the *inordinate* favoring of any species over any other species. And what is the theological objection to theological speciesism? We might speak of two forms of theological speciesism and two concomitant theological failures. Inordinate over-concern for any species is, among other things, a form of idolatry. Inordinate under-concern (i.e., a lack of appropriate concern for any species) is a rejection of God's good creation and thus a different kind of failure in the Christian's worship and praise of God. Thus we arrive at a definition of theological speciesism, namely *a failure to see the variety of non-human animals the way God sees them; that is, failing to see them as creatures of God who manifest God's goodness and give praise to God in their flourishing as creatures of diverse natures.*

Having furnished working definitions of speciesism and theological speciesism, we can turn to typical responses to this critique in Catholic moral thought.

[3] By referring to "kind" I do not mean to be taking any position on the controverted questions regarding the existence of "natural kinds" versus merely species (i.e., interbreeding populations), nor what might constitutes an appropriate definition of either. For a good introduction to the issues, see Stephen R. L. Clark, "Is humanity a natural kind?" in *The Political Animal: Biology, Ethics, and Politics* (London: Routledge, 1999), 40-58.

Surveying the Scene: Catholic Moral Theology on Speciesism

The first thing to say about defenses of speciesism in Catholic moral theology is that they are hard to find. Looking at a range of "introduction to moral theology" textbooks (and I won't mention all kinds of names, except for the otherwise excellent *Introducing Moral Theology*[4] by my good friend Bill Mattison), there is no reference to concern for non-human animals as an ethical issue. Nor do animals constitute a topic of concern in a variety of collections of essays on the Catholic moral life (and again I won't mention names, except for the other excellent collection *Gathered for the Journey*[5] edited by my friends David McCarthy and Therese Lysaught). Intrinsic concern for animals as a moral topic also do not make it into the introductions to health care ethics and biomedicine in Catholic moral theology over thirty-plus years, not even making it into the recent introductory text by my good friend Nicanor Austriaco.[6] Animals as a moral topic also do not make the cut in comprehensive magisterial documents of the Catholic Church on social ethics, such as *The Compendium of the Social Doctrine of the Church* (although it has a long section on the environment).[7] Even my friend Tobias Winright's wonderful recent edited volume *Green Discipleship* is silent on the status of non-human animals.[8]

The point of the previous paragraph is not to be "chummy" with, nor to offend and annoy a variety of my friends and colleagues in the guild of moral theology. I admire and respect all the books I have mentioned above. And I could have easily referenced a large variety of well-known or classic texts in the field by other colleagues and acquaintances in the field. For, to put it more bluntly, overviews of Catholic moral theology (either of the discipline as a whole or of its major sub-fields) in this last generation have ignored both the general issue of human responsibilities to non-human animals, and the specific issue of animal cruelty.[9] This even seems true of Catholic texts giving a

---

[4] William C. Mattison III, *Introducing Moral Theology: True Happiness and the Virtues* (Grand Rapids: Brazos Press, 2008).

[5] David Matzko McCarthy and M. Therese Lysaught. *Gathered for the Journey: Moral Theology in Catholic Perspective* (Grand Rapids: Eerdmans, 2007).

[6] Nicanor Pier Giorgio Austriaco. *Biomedicine and Beatitude: An Introduction to Catholic Bioethics* (Washington, DC: The Catholic University of America Press, 2011).

[7] Pontifical Council for Justice and Peace, *Compendium of the Social Doctrine of the Church* (Washington, DC: United States Conference of Catholic Bishops, 2005).

[8] The exception is an essay in the inter-religious section of the book by a Jewish author. See Tobias Winright, ed., *Green Discipleship: Catholic Theological Ethics and the Environment* (Winona: Anselm Academic, 2011).

[9] That of course does not mean no Catholic moral theologians have ever addressed the topic. In the 1960s Justus George Lawler wrote a series of articles on non-human animals, including "Towards a Theology of Animals," which appeared in *The Range*

comprehensive view of ecological or environmental ethics. As for the very few Catholic moral theologians who do write about animal ethics, it is its own little area, with hardly any integration into the larger field.[10] I am very pleased to note that this very issue of the *Journal of Moral Theology*—both in terms of the *Journal's* willingness to devote this issue to this topic and the fact that a number of moral theologians are contributing to it—is a sign that things are changing.

In light of the fact that Catholic moral theology has not even seen the need to discuss or justify its ignoring the various moral issues to do with our relationships with other animals, whether it has to do with eating them and wearing their skins, or experimenting on them or keeping them in zoos or as pets, or even the egregious and cruel ways so many animals are treated in factory farming, one wonders if "speciesist" is the apt term for the current state of Catholic moral theology. When it comes to non-human animals and Catholic moral theology, moral nihilism and/or moral indifference seem to be the apt descriptors. Non-human animals are not even on the margins! Hence the title of the session we organized at the SCE in January of 2103.

If we moral theologians reflect on the fact of the moral vacuum in the field with regard to this topic, this is really astounding. For example, in 2011 in her remarks at the Catholic Mass at the SCE, Catholic moral theologian Christine Gudorf spoke of the number of her students who have become vegetarians for ethical reasons. Her experience is no doubt typical for those who teach undergraduates or seminarians. Despite our apparent silence, our students are discovering that the treatment of non-human animals is a serious moral issue. Popular books and films like *Fast Food Nation*, *The Omnivore's Dilemma*, and *Food Inc.*, just to name a few, parade the ethical issues before us. And yet we as a discipline have been almost entirely silent in this past generation. In fact, at a recent international gathering of Catholic moral theologians, the entrée of choice at the closing banquet was veal (of all meats!).[11] (Charles Camosy and I were awaiting a follow-up of *pâté de foie gras* served as an *amuse-bouche*.) How as a discipline have we managed to be blind to this? As such we fail our students. And this is particularly awful considering that this past generation has seen the

---

of Commitment: Essays of a Conservative Liberal (Milwaukee: Bruce Publishing Co., 1969). And over the last 20 years an occasional article or book has appeared that takes up aspects of the question—see the next footnote. My point is that the field has up until very recently not recognized the topic as part of its overall field of concern.

[10] Besides the contributors to this volume, Catholic moral theologians who have occasionally presented or published in the area include William French, James Gaffney, Elizabeth Groppe, Beth Haile, Deborah Jones, Fergus Kerr, Jame Schaefer, Vincent Twomey, and Donna Yarri.

[11] This took place at the final banquet of the international meeting of *Catholic Moral Theologians in the World Church* in Trento, Italy in 2010.

explosion of factory farming in the West, with cruel treatment of animals on a scale and to a degree unlike ever before seen in our world.

And the great irony in all this is that for all their faults (and for all the ways in which some contemporary Catholic moral theologians denigrate them), the pre-Vatican II moral manuals typically included a section on human responsibilities to non-human animals. Although the manuals indicated that cruelty to non-human animals could be wrong for instrumental reasons (i.e., we damage our character or are more likely to be cruel to other humans if we are cruel to animals), they also typically indicate that non-human animals are God's creatures with their own dignity, and cruelty to them is an offence against God's providential concern for all of God's creatures. For example, in his *Introduction to Moral Theology*, Karl Hörmann's discussion of non-human animals begins with an extended meditation on the intrinsic goodness of non-human animals. He begins by noting that "[a]ll creation is destined by a loving God for transformation.... The more powerfully the sonship of God is realized, so much the more certain is the guarantee that all creation will find its meaning in God's glory and in the transfiguration which comes from this."[12] Furthermore, when Hörmann discusses the moral treatment of animals, he notes that cruelty to animals can constitute grave sin, because it "offends against the grave obligation of love for God's creatures," and also "ruins the character of the person who indulges in it."[13] So this is one question where post-Vatican II Catholic moralists need to catch up to their pre-Vatican II predecessors.[14]

A Typology of Defenses of Speciesism

While moral theologians have typically not taken up a defense of speciesism, Catholic philosophers have,[15] and their defenses of speciesism fall into three main categories: a) there are *zero-sum defenders*, that begin with the assumption that greater concern for animals

---

[12] Karl Hörmann, *An Introduction to Moral Theology* (Westminister, MD: Newman Press, 1961), 273.

[13] Hörmann, *Introduction*, 275.

[14] It is also worth noting that in Hörmann's preface, he explains that as a "handbook" in moral theology "the presentation had to be concise... and some of the less important problems had to be omitted altogether" (v). It is thus all the more notable that Hörmann includes a four page section on non-humans in his 276 page introductory text.

[15] I do not mean to infer that *many* Catholic philosophers took up a response. For example, although ethical questions about animals were widely in the news by the mid-1970s, both because of the chimpanzee language experiments of the late 1960s and early 1970s, and also because of Singer and other philosophical animal advocates, in 1985 Catholic philosopher R.J. McLaughlin could write, "Accelerated research into animal behavior has brought us to see many 'brute' animals, as much less brutish than we previous thought, and much more like us. Our fondness for animals has grown proportionately, as has the suspicion that the radically different way in which we treat man and beast may not be justified.... I invite you to join me in pressing with St.

means less concern for human beings; b) there are the *rationalist defenders*, which focus on (typically a Thomist) account of rationality (or since the 1960s, often of linguistic ability in relation to rationality) to draw a relatively sharp line between human and non-human animals; c) there are *abstract concern defenders*, that acknowledge the recent ethological advances in understanding a variety of species, and for that or other reasons acknowledge we should have significant concern for the welfare of non-human animals. However, these "abstract concern defenders" fail to engage in the kind of casuistry necessary to provide and implement the practical guidance necessary to actually impact our lives with regard to the treatment of non-human animals.

Zero-sum defenses

Zero-sum defenses are typically reactionary, preoccupied with countering viewpoints of philosophers who argue for a version of animal rights. As one would expect, many Catholic philosophers over the years have been eager to respond to Peter Singer's views on the moral treatment of non-human animals, especially in relation to his view on the moral treatment of some human animals! Furthermore, as is widely known, since some of the more extreme animal rights viewpoints give equal or greater moral value to some other mammals than to some human beings (e.g., human infants, very young children, or human beings who have severe mental impairments), it is not surprising that these arguments elicited strong reactions. Thus it entirely predictable that a typical response to Singer's arguments would be to argue for inherent and universal human dignity, and to make arguments as to why all human beings (and typically only human beings) have this dignity. If Singer was going to provoke, and in some instances give more value to a non-human animal life than to a human life, the zero-sum defenders could be expected to respond in kind, arguing not only that all human beings are not only worth more than any non-human animals, but that they are worth incomparably more. This is the heart of the zero-sum defense. Any concern for animals seems to lessen or relativize concern for humans.

The fundamental problem with the zero-sum response is that it missed the overarching point of philosophers like Singer, Regan, et al., who are ultimately and primarily arguing for concern for non-human animals. We can certainly commend those zero-sum defenders for advocating universal human dignity. But in responding as they did the zero-sum defenders typically bypass the question of appropriate

Thomas whether there is anything about man, in contrast to other animals especially, that justifies the favored treatment that we accord him.... *People sympathetic to Thomas's way of doing philosophy have been curiously silent on this question* (italics added)," R.J. McLaughlin, "Men, Animals and Personhood," *Proceedings of the American Catholic Philosophical Association* Vol. 59 (1985), 166-7.

concern for non-human animals in order to get right to the conclusion that advocating for human dignity requires them to disparage all non-human animals. Ironically, I suspect many of the zero-sum defenders do not actually believe this in practice. Likely many of them have pets whom they love, and whom they think deserve appropriate treatment. And most likely think that zoo animals ought to be treated well, and cruelty to non-human animals should be avoided when possible, and wild animals should receive some habitat protection and so on.

The irony is that these otherwise sensible Catholic philosophers allowed Singer to set the terms of the question, and were thus lured into the *reductio ad absurdum* of the radicalized zero-sum viewpoint. Latent (if not baldly stated) by the zero-sum speciesists is a doctrine of "human exceptionalism." And so it turns out that the zero-sum defenders simply have no interest in giving serious thought to understanding (nor morally evaluating) the significance of the natures or rational capabilities of any particular species of non-human animal.[16]

What's problematic about this human exceptionalism? Isn't this typical of the Catholic tradition to think of only human beings as persons and thus worthy of moral concern and protection? Well, no, it isn't "the" Catholic tradition, although dominant strands of it, especially under the influence of the Cartesian view of animals, have come very close to that.

But beyond that, it is also the case that for decades Catholic philosophers have been willing to consider attributing "personhood" and moral concern to non-human beings. But this openness to attributing personhood to non-humans has centered on discussions of the possibility of extending personhood and attendant rights and protections to Martians or other intelligent extra-terrestrials (or even androids) if one should arrive on earth or otherwise make contact with us earthlings.[17]

---

[16] Many, many examples could be given. John Finnis dismisses "animal rights" in one paragraph in *Natural Law and Natural Rights* (Oxford: Clarendon Press, 1980), 194-5. He says nothing about what would be appropriate concern for non-human animals, his only apparent interest being to refute Singer. A more recent and telling example is Christopher Kaczor's "Notes on Philosophy and Theology," *National Catholic Bioethics Quarterly*, Vol. 10, no. 4 (Winter 2010), 799-805. Kaczor's article begins by noting it is about animal rights, which involves questions like "Is eating meat morally permissible? Can hunting be justified? Do sentient animals deserve greater consideration than non-sentient human beings?"(799). But then Kaczor goes on to indicate he will in fact only discuss whether "species membership is relevant to ethical judgment" (799). Like many other Catholic philosophers, Kaczor is lured into Peter Singer's intellectual framework, spending the beginning of his article attempting to refute Singer, and then allowing his whole article to become an extended polemic against Singer and his intellectual allies in defending human dignity. In this article ostensibly about non-human animals, Kaczor manages to say not a single word about how it is appropriate or inappropriate to treat non-human animals, much less even begin to address his own opening questions about meat eating or hunting.

[17] See, for example, Philip Devine, *The Ethics of Homicide* (Ithica: Cornell University Press, 1978), 53ff. Discussions about Martians/aliens as "persons" have been a stock

That being the case, it seems that the zero-sum defenders should in principle be open to the fact that there may be other intelligent and moral "alien" species, species that could possibly be living unrecognized in our homes, or in our zoos, or in our laboratories, or in our abattoirs, or in the wild. And yet, as noted above, the zero-sum defenders have not been interested in exploring whether there might be one or more other earthly species of being more intelligent and/or more moral than we have heretofore realized.

Rationalist defenses

The second type of speciesist among Catholic intellectuals provides rationalist defenses, and they vary tremendously. The clumsiest ones simply assert a sharp rational/irrational distinction, uncritically taking over terminology derived from centuries past. Their crude generalizations and stereotypes about non-human animals are so foreign to the reality of the diversity of God's creatures, it leads one to wonder if some of them have ever actually met a live animal!

However, the typical rationalist defense of speciesism among Catholic moralists follows an authentic strand of Thomistic thought. Aquinas clearly believed that humans were the only rational animals, and combined with his view of the hierarchical order of nature, claimed that non-human animals were for the use of human beings.[18]

---

example for philosophers discussing the nature and meaning of personhood, particularly in relation to the philosophical debates over abortion since the early 1970s. For a rather different book on theology and "E.T.'s," see Thomas O'Meara, O.P., *Vast Universe: Extraterrestrials and Christian Revelation* (Collegeville: Liturgical Press, 2012).

[18] The first of these two viewpoints, that humans are the only rational animals, is almost universally held by Thomists, and many offer sophisticated versions of it. A classic Thomist argument for this is Mortimer Adler, *The Difference of Man and the Difference it Makes* (New York: Holt, Rinehart, and Winston, 1967). An accessible yet sophisticated exponent of this viewpoint is Herbert McCabe, who expounds versions of it in "Sense and Sensibility" in *God Still Matters* (New York: Continuum, 2002), in "Organism, Language, and Grace" and "Animals and Us" in *The Good Life: Ethics and the Pursuit of Happiness* (London: Continuum, 2005) and in "Sensations, Language, and Individuals" in *On Aquinas* (London: Burns & Oates, 2008).

The second of these viewpoints, that because non-human animals are irrational they are thus "lesser" beings and thus for the use of human beings, is often stated but rarely argued. For example Peter Drum, after discussing at length the distinction between rational humans and all other irrational animals, quotes Aquinas that "'less perfect things are ordered to the more perfect' (Aquinas, ST, II-II, 64.2), so there is nothing wrong with persons using animals to satisfy personal needs and to achieve personal benefits." See Peter Drum, "Aquinas and the Moral Status of Animals," *American Catholic Philosophical Quarterly*, Vol. 66, no. 4 (1992), 487. Having quoted Aquinas, Drum seems satisfied merely to say "this seems right as the well-being of fully-fledged moral patients is clearly more important than the well-being of those that are not" (487). That may all be true, but from that does not follow that humans can use animals for almost whatever purposes they desire. The point being highlighted

This is not the whole story of Aquinas's views on non-human animals and their capacities,[19] but it is widespread in the tradition and suffices for many rationalist defenders of speciesism in the Catholic tradition.

It should also be noted that being a defender of the Thomistic view that "rationality" in the Thomistic sense is unique to human beings does not in itself make one a speciesist. Countless religious and secular advocates of concern for non-human animals hold this view or a close variant of it.[20] What typically makes a rationalist defender of speciesism a speciesist is their holding a related Thomistic viewpoint, namely that sub-rational creatures have no (or inconsequential) intrinsic goodness and may be used willy-nilly by human beings for almost any purpose.[21] Having said that, current research in ethology on the social skills, and on the emotional, intellectual, and/or even moral capacities of a variety of animals (e.g., primates, canids, cetaceans, corvids, and cephalopods) makes the continued use of traditional generalizations about the "rationality" or lack thereof in all "non-human animals" increasingly intellectually irresponsible.

However, recent developments in Thomistic scholarship are opening new possibilities for a better understanding of non-human animals. First, the recent attention to the emotions and sense appetites in Thomas Aquinas is very important, since that is a focus on those central characteristics of human beings that, as Aquinas notes, humans share with higher non-human animals. Although Thomas says that human beings transform their passions in relation to their rational will, Thomas also acknowledges that the "estimative sense" in non-human animals constitutes a kind of quasi-rationality. However, Thomists

---

here is that Drum (like most other rational defense speciesists) apparently sees no need to argue or justify this view.

[19] I have elaborated on Aquinas's views on animals and human animality in "Toward a Thomistic Theology of Animality" in *Creaturely Theology: On God, Humans and Other Animals*, ed. Celia Deane-Drummond and David Clough (London: SCM Press, 2009), 21-40. A balanced overview treatment of Aquinas's views on animals can be found in chapter 1 of Ryan Patrick McLoughlin, *Christian Theology and the Status of Animals: The Dominant Tradition and Its Alternatives* (London: Palgrave/MacMillan, 2014).

[20] Including, it would seem, Frans De Waal. When discussing his three-level account of morality, De Waal gets to the third level and says, "Perhaps this reflects just our current state of knowledge, but I know of no parallels in animals for moral reasoning.... The desire for an internally consistent moral framework is uniquely human. We are the only ones to worry about why we think what we think.... I consider this level of morality, with its desire for consistency and 'disinterestedness', and its careful weighing of what one did against what one could or should have done, uniquely human. Even though it never fully transcends primate social motives, our internal dialogue nevertheless lifts moral behavior to a level of abstraction and self-reflections unheard of before our species entered the evolutionary scene." Frans De Waal, *Primates and Philosophers: How Morality Evolved* (Princeton: Princeton University Press, 2006), 174-5.

[21] See the second viewpoint discussed in footnote 18 above.

have not done the work to go beyond Thomas and investigate with empirical evidence how the estimative sense coordinates the senses in particular higher non-human animals.

Thus, the most promising work is being done by those who seek to bring together contemporary work in ethology with philosophical reflection on the sense appetites to potentially better understand the varieties of intelligence in a variety of non-human animal species. We see a brief example of this in Alasdair MacIntyre's *Dependent Rational Animals*. However, although MacIntyre discusses dolphins for a number of chapters in that book, MacIntyre in fact appears uninterested in dolphins for their own sake (at least in that book), merely using his reflections on dolphins to instruct his readers about the significance of a particular aspect (that is, the bodily aspect) of human life.[22] What we need, and what the final section of this article calls for, are *theological ethologists*, that is, moral theologians who develop a deep understanding of a particular (e.g., dolphin or chimpanzee) species and integrate that with their theological understanding of God's intrinsic concern for that particular (e.g., dolphin or chimpanzee) species. This could and would take moral theologians beyond the facile generalized arguments about sentience and rationality and actually begin to understand the particular good of real dolphins and real chimpanzees, and make concrete proposals about promoting the good (or at least avoiding continued egregious harm) towards these species in relation to their specific good. At the very least moral theologians and philosophers would then be able to speak intelligently about the intellectual and practical capacities of the particular species, and perhaps develop an analogous natural law understanding of the flourishing that should properly be ascribed to these dolphins and/or chimpanzees. What we need are modern day St. Alberts, who like Albert in his thirteenth century *On Animals*, attempt to bring together the best of currently existing ethology and theology to understand the natures and destinies of particular non-human species.

Abstract concern defenses

Finally, there are the *abstract concern* defenders of speciesism.[23]

---

[22] Alasdair MacIntyre, *Dependent Rational Animals* (London: Open Court Press, 1999). MacIntyre discusses dolphins (and other higher animals including primates) in chapters 2-6, but then at the beginning of chapter 7 suddenly makes a transition to discussing the development of human children. With the exception of occasionally recapitulating his overall argument, MacIntyre does not return to discussing non-human animals for the rest of the book.

[23] A most interesting analysis of arguments around the treatment of non-human animals is the philosopher Philip Devine's 1978 article "The Moral Basis of Vegetarianism," *Philosophy* Vol. 53 (1978), 481-505. This highly clever article takes up and dispatches an extraordinarily large number of relevant arguments in a highly compressed manner. However, while Devine finally concludes that the treatment of non-

The philosophers and theologians in this category typically acknowledge the intrinsic goodness of non-human animals, that we have moral responsibilities in our treatment of them, and that we should be concerned for their welfare. As such these thinkers are not explicit but implicit speciesists. Why are they implicit speciesists? Because while they acknowledge the grave evils that humans can and do perpetuate with regard to non-human animals, they fail (either completely or adequately) to engage in the casuistry necessary to show that their concern is real and not merely notional. For the evils done by humans to non-humans animals—most egregiously (but not exclusively) in factory farming—require moral philosophers and theologians to engage in the type of casuistry that can suggest the kinds of changes necessary to overcome or at least relieve aspects of these evils.

Interestingly, of the few Catholic moralists over the last generation who acknowledge the intrinsic goodness of non-human animals as creatures of God, and thus acknowledge that we have some responsibilities to them, some seem to do so in continuity with and almost out of deference to the older tradition of the manuals and their inclusion of the treatment of non-human animals as a moral question. So for example, Germain Grisez acknowledges that we should not be cruel to animals without good reason, but does not spell out what constitutes "good reason." Furthermore, the limited amount of casuistry he does never requires him to take a particular ethical stand regarding a minimum of respectful treatment of any non-human animal. Since he never takes up paradigmatic cases of animal cruelty like factory farming as is overwhelming practiced in the West and now also in the second and third world, he is never required to establish any norm resolutely advocating for basic concern for the welfare of non-human animals. Having said that, the fact that Grisez even includes the treatment of non-human animals as a moral question in his work and engages in some casuistry what is involved is a credit to him and serves as at least as a starting point for more developed and adequate treatments of the subject.

From this very brief typology, we can conclude that as of right now, the Catholic moral tradition has almost nothing to contribute constructively to reflecting on the moral status of particular species of non-human animals, especially in light of modern ethology. This is a very unfortunate state of affairs that we can hope will change in the

---

human animals is a morally serious question, he proposes no solutions or guidance regarding the societal issues.

Germain Grisez takes up the intrinsic significance of non-human animals and their moral treatment in a few places, albeit briefly and without enthusiasm. See Grisez, *The Way of the Lord Jesus Vol. 2: Living a Christian Life* (Quincy, IL: Franciscan Press, 1993), 782-9. Grisez also takes up questions related to the moral treatment of animals in Grisez, *The Way of the Lord Jesus Vol. 3: Difficult Moral Questions* (Quincy, IL: Franciscan Press, 1997), 419-25.

coming years. For I believe it is essential that as our contemporary society evolves in light of new knowledge about the emotional, moral, and intellectual capacities of cetaceans, great apes, elephants, pigs and various other species, that Catholic moral theology be able to contextualize this new knowledge for contemporary society in a way consonant with an authentic Catholic vision of the world.

NON-HUMAN ANIMALS IN *THE CATECHISM OF THE CATHOLIC CHURCH*

In the midst of the deafening silence of post-Vatican II Catholic moral theology on animals, there is one very significant, albeit puzzling Catholic teaching on non-human animals. Sections 2415-2418 of the 1997 *Catechism of the Catholic Church* read as follows:

> Respect for the integrity of creation
>
> 2415 The seventh commandment enjoins respect for the integrity of creation. Animals, like plants and inanimate beings, are by nature destined for the common good of past, present, and future humanity. (Cf. Gen 128-31) Use of the mineral, vegetable, and animal resources of the universe cannot be divorced from respect for moral imperatives. Man's dominion over inanimate and other living beings granted by the Creator is not absolute; it is limited by concern for the quality of life of his neighbor, including generations to come; it requires a religious respect for the integrity of creation. (Cf. CA 37-38)
>
> 2416 Animals are God's creatures. He surrounds them with his providential care. By their mere existence they bless him and give him glory. (Mt 6:26; Dan 3:79-81) Thus men owe them kindness. We should recall the gentleness with which saints like St. Francis of Assisi or St. Philip Neri treated animals.
>
> 2417 God entrusted animals to the stewardship of those whom he created in his own image. (Cf. Gen 2:19-20; 9:1-4) Hence it is legitimate to use animals for food and clothing. They may be domesticated to help man in his work and leisure. Medical and scientific experimentation on animals is a morally acceptable practice, if it remains within reasonable limits and contributes to caring for or saving human lives.
>
> 2418 It is contrary to human dignity to cause animals to suffer or die needlessly. It is likewise unworthy to spend money on them that should as a priority go to the relief of human misery. One can love animals; one should not direct to them the affection due only to persons.

The first thing to note is that the *Catechism* treats moral questions involving non-human animals under the heading "Respect for the integrity of creation," which is part of a larger section on respecting the property of others (which is in turn part of a discussion of the seventh command against stealing). This is the first sign that we can expect the

Catechism's moral analysis of the treatment of non-human animals to follow that of the moral manuals, which also tended to locate discussions of non-human animals under the seventh commandment against stealing.

My summary evaluation of the *Catechism* is that it does not have one clearly consistent view on the moral treatment of non-human animals. Rather, it seems to have a variety of views that are at best in tension with one another, and perhaps even incompatible with each other. While some aspects of the teaching are speciesist, other aspects provide a wonderful starting point for Catholic moral and theological reflection on non-human animals. And still other aspects of it are mystifying, leaving the reader with little guidance on applying the teaching. Let us take each in turn.

Since the *Catechism's* discussion of animals appears in the section on the commandment not to steal and to respect the property of other human beings, it would seem to have speciesist assumptions, namely that non-human animals are the property of humans. And this reading is reinforced by lines like "Animals… are by nature destined for the common good of… humanity" (no. 2415).

On the other hand, paragraph 2416 emphasizes a seemingly different message, emphasizing God's love and concern for his creatures (i.e., they belong fundamentally to God, not to humans). It notes that non-human animals bless God by the intrinsic goodness of their existence and flourishing. As noted above, here the *Catechism* provides a solid basis for a truly theocentric perspective on non-human animals. And if one focuses on paragraph 2416, one can easily interpret the context of this section rather differently. In other words, the context for the discussion of non-humans animals is not what belongs to humans, but rather what belongs to God. Furthermore, paragraph 2416 assigns moral duties to humans with regard to the care of other animals and also reminds us of the saints whose love of non-human animals is to be imitated.

Finally, section 2418 seems to take a still different approach, apparently giving only instrumental reasons for not being cruel to animals ("contrary to human dignity"). But what of the God-given intrinsic goodness of these creatures? Or of humans as stewards who should reflect God's providential care of other animals? The different paragraphs seem so different in substance and tone that one can't help but speculate if, like the book of Genesis, this small section of the catechism had multiple authors (or editors), whose differing views have been left standing side by side.

Paragraph 2418 also gives mystifying moral guidance. With regard to its "no needless suffering" injunction, what constitutes "needlessly" causing an animal to suffer or die? If one reads only no. 2415 before reading that, almost any reason would seem to do, since they are destined for the good of humans. But if one only reads no. 2416 before reading it, it would seem one would need a very strong reason for causing an animal to suffer or die. One fears that as stated these paragraphs seem more likely to reinforce a person's existing views about harming animals (almost whatever they are) than lead to a new one.

With regard to the "give priority to human misery" injunction, which is presumably referring to pets (though one could interpret it as applying to zoos? or wildlife refuges? or efforts to reintroduce species to where they are endangered or extinct?), its language is puzzlingly strong. Is it a rhetorical way of saying "don't treat your pets luxuriously"? For those more ascetically inclined—or for those who do not like other animals—it could plausibly be interpreted as discouraging almost any spending of money on non-human animals. But that interpretation would seem to easily lead to the utilitarian *reductio ad absurdum* that one should not spend money on anything less urgent than the relief of human misery. So it remains at least somewhat obscure as a piece of moral guidance.

The final unclear directive is that while it is fine to love animals, do not give them affection due only to (human) persons. For this begs the question as to what affection is due only to human persons. Again, one puzzles to conjure up the kind of scenario envisioned by the authors of the *Catechism*. Is this a reproach to those poor souls who prefer the exclusive company of their companion animals to any interaction with other human beings? Or exclusively devote their lives to their companion animals? Again, while the exhortation initially sounds compelling, one searches for an appropriate application.

So what do we conclude about this section of the *Catechism*? Part of me wants to be cheeky and say that this is what we should expect when Catholic moral theology has had practically nothing to say on a moral topic in the thirty years prior to the *Catechism*! And in fact, when read along aside a variety of the pre-Vatican II moral manuals, much of what the *Catechism* says is simply repeating that teaching. But the *Catechism*, while maintaining much of that older teaching (particularly its concern about those who lavish too much attention on non-human animals), also adds a rather different emphasis, in terms of the legitimacy of love for animals, in emphasizing God's providential concern for other species, and in highlighting the lives of the saints who have shown love and compassion for non-human animals.

I have argued elsewhere[24] that at the time of Vatican II Catholic moral theology more generally was in what MacIntyre calls an epistemological crisis.[25] I believe this small section of the Catechism gives

[24] See John Berkman, "How Important is the Doctrine of Double Effect? Contextualizing the Controversy," *Christian Bioethics* Vol. 3, no. 2 (1997), especially 92-5.

[25] According to MacIntyre, the signs that a mode of enquiry (such as the Catholic moral tradition's thought on non-human animals) is in epistemological crisis are when "by its own standard of progress it ceases to make progress. Its hitherto trusted methods of enquiry have become sterile. Conflicts over rival answers to key questions can

us good reason to believe that there is an epistemological crisis in the tradition's reflection on this topic. The older manualist approach to thinking about non-human animals is no longer sufficient, and in itself does not have the resources for a renewed theological and moral approach to the subject. And yet, the new elements of Catholic teaching as embodied in the *Catechism* have not yet been sufficiently developed to signal a clear way forward for the Catholic moral tradition's thought on non-human animals. Thus, the framework for the moral treatment of non-human animals in the *Catechism* shows cracks and fissures. The question for us at present is thus: What is needed from moral theology so that in a future generation and with a future *Catechism*, something more intellectually coherent and morally compelling could be offered?

From Theological Speciesism to Theological Ethology

What is the kind of work that needs to be done to avoid theological speciesism, that is, to learn to see all the other animals God has placed with humans on earth as God sees them, and to learn how to live as harmoniously as possible with them? The following would seem to be at least some of the tasks that require further work and reflection by Catholic moral theologians.

Humans as animals

First, there is much work to be done by moral theologians to overcome the problematic aspects of the crude binary between humans and all other animals. Of course, there are perfectly legitimate biological reasons (e.g., mammalian species tend to be primarily interested in their own), legal reasons (e.g., we wish to maintain distinct levels of legal protection to all human beings) and theological reasons (e.g., God assigns to humans a variety of unique tasks) to maintain interest in and language about that which is distinctively human. That is not under question. What is problematic is what seems to be a distinctively modern binary between humans and "animals" as the great divide in terms of moral concern, as if humans are not in fact animals and "animals" refers to all other sentient creatures which are not human beings. In a public lecture David Clough noted that in the King James Bible there is no term for "animal" as it is now commonly used, that is, a term referring to all other sentient creatures. The ancients and

no longer be settled rationally. Moreover, it may indeed happen that the use of the methods of enquiry and of the forms of argument, by means of which rational progress had been achieved so far, begins to have the effect of increasingly disclosing new inadequacies, hitherto unrecognized incoherences, and new problems for the solution of which there seem to be insufficient or no resources within the established fabric of belief." Alasdair MacIntyre, *Whose Justice? Which Rationality?* (Notre Dame: University of Notre Dame Press, 1988), 361-2.

medievals all recognized that we humans are also animals. For example, St. Albert and St. Thomas refer to human beings as animals on dozens of occasions. Whereas in former ages "acting like a beast" was to act according to one's lower nature, in modern parlance it more often than not means that is one is not acting like a human being at all. Since the view that humans are not animals is now so well-entrenched in our thought patterns and our language, a major first step is a deconstructive project of unmasking the modern facade that humans are not also animals.

Rejecting cognitive parsimony

Jane Goodall and Frans De Waal have taught us that chimpanzees live in close knit societies, and yet there are bouts of discord among them. De Waal recounts an anecdote about the time he finally noticed a striking long-term pattern among chimpanzees in which former opponents in a squabble were "attracted to each other like magnets."[26] De Waal goes on to discuss the patterns of embracing, kissing, and grooming that so often occurred with former opponents in a fight, sometimes immediately after the fight, but at other times hours later. Furthermore, conflicts between two individual chimpanzees impacted the whole group, with tension and hesitancy in the group until the former combatants made affectionate overtures to one another. De Waal says:

> The obvious word to describe this phenomenon is reconciliation, but I have heard people object to it on the grounds that by choosing such terms chimpanzees are unnecessarily humanized. Why not call it something neutral like "first post-conflict contact," because after all that is what it is? Out of the same desire for objectivity, kissing could be called "mouth-mouth contact," embrace "arms-around-shoulder," face "snout," and hand "front paw." I am inclined to take the motives put forward in favor of dehumanized terminology with a pinch of salt. Is it not an attempt to veil in words the mirror that chimpanzees hold up to us? Might we not be sticking out heads in the sand to preserve our need for dignity?[27]

This brings us to the point that all observers of chimpanzees bring their pre-conceptions to their observations. Those more willing to see continuity and analogies between human and chimpanzee behavior tend to appeal to the principle of evolutionary parsimony. De Waal explains that evolutionary parsimony is the principle that if closely related species act similarly, then we should presume that the underlying sensory, emotional, and cognitive processes that lead to those actions are also

---

[26] Frans De Waal, *Chimpanzee Politics: Power and Sex Among Apes, 25th Anniversary Edition* (Baltimore: Johns Hopkins University Press, 2007), 27.
[27] De Waal, *Chimpanzee Politics*, 28.

similar.[28] On the other hand, those who tend to resist seeing continuity between chimpanzee and human behavior also appeal to a principle of parsimony, sometimes called cognitive parsimony, namely that one should not attribute cognitive processes to another creature without overwhelming evidence, presumably because for so long the reigning scientific doctrine has been that other animals do not think.

But what, one may ask, is problematic about holding to the principle of cognitive parsimony? Is it not the right approach to doubt that animals can think unless we can clearly infer it from their behavior? MacIntyre argues that this is exactly the wrong approach to take if one wants to understand the nature and capacities of chimpanzees or other higher animals. (MacIntyre focuses on dolphins and other cetaceans.) Contrary to those philosophers deeply troubled by the problem of "other minds" (i.e., how can one *know* if any other human beings actually have minds) and those who apply the "principle of parsimony" to what otherwise appears to be signs of theoretical or practical intelligence in chimpanzees and/or other higher animals, MacIntyre argues that human beings come to essential understandings of themselves and other human and non-human animals *only* through pre-reflective engagement with and experience of them. According to MacIntyre, *pre-reflective* interpretive experience is absolutely crucial in coming to understand the practical reasoning of both human children and other intelligent animals.[29] Without such interpretative experience, MacIntyre says, "We would be unable to ascribe thoughts and feelings to others, whether human infants or dogs or whatever."[30]

In other words, we can only come to understand the capacities of chimpanzees by extensive interaction with them and wise interpretation of what we experience with them, that is, the kind of interaction to which ethologists like Jane Goodall and Frans De Waal and Sue Savage-Rumbaugh have devoted much of their lives. I say "ethologists like Jane Goodall and Frans De Waal and Sue Savage-Rumbaugh" because we should be careful not to give equal weight to the experience of some who extensively interact with chimpanzees—that is, those who for one reason or another are captured by a pre-existing account of what chimpanzees "should" or "should not" be able to do.[31]

---

[28] De Waal, *Primates and Philosophers*, 61-2.

[29] MacIntyre also refers to this "pre-reflective experience" as "non-inferential knowledge," by which he means knowledge that arises from entering into a relationship of responsive activity with the other human or chimpanzee (or, for example, elephant or dolphin).

[30] MacIntyre, *Dependent Rational Animals*, 24. For an excellent effort by a philosopher to bring pre-reflective experience to bear on his understanding of his dog, see Raimond Gaita, *The Philosopher's Dog* (New York: Random House, 2005)

[31] It is not just philosophers who are likely to be captured by modern epistemological skepticism about chimpanzees (or a huge range of other species) having feelings

Evolution and continuity in ethics

A number of moral theologians (e.g., Celia Deane-Drummond, John Mahoney, and Stephen Pope) have already done important work on the significance of evolutionary theory for understanding proto-moral and moral behavior in theological perspective. To do that they engage the work of anthropologists, paleontologists and ethologists to understand the origins of morality not only in our hominid and hominoid precursors, but also for signs of proto-morality and/or morality in various other primates.

In so doing, these moral theologians take one side in an age-old division in thinking about ethics. While an oversimplification, one can divide philosophical and theological thinking about the origins of morality into two camps. There is the continuity camp, which understands that at least some elements of human morality are on a continuum with and/or develop out of characteristics that humans share with our hominid precursors and/or the precursors of other primates. In this camp one will find ancients and medievals like Aristotle and Aquinas, enlightenment empiricists like David Hume, and Darwinians like Edward Westermarck. On the other hand, there are those who believe that morality is something in humans that reflects a fundamental disjunction from all other creatures. In this camp one will find ancients like the Gnostics, medieval and reformation divine command theorists, rationalists like Rene Descartes and Immanuel Kant, and Darwinians like Thomas Huxley.

It is important to emphasize that the continuity viewpoint by no means arises with evolutionary theory. For example, St. Albert has an extended discussion of the bodily form of the human animal and its perfection and clearly relates the human's rational ability to its bodily form. In Albert's discussion of various other animals, he proceeds with the view that the degree of bodily likeness to humans is associated with the degree of mental likeness to humans. Thus, in his discussion of pygmies and monkeys, he classifies them in such a way that the descending scale of physical likeness to humans corresponds with their mental likeness.[32]

---

and/or thoughts. As I noted in my discussion of zero-sum speciesists, some see moral concern as a zero-sum game, that if it is to be extended to chimpanzees it must detract from what is accorded human beings. (Celia Deane-Drummond also takes up this problematic in her essay in this issue of the *Journal of Moral Theology*.) As I note below in discussing anthropocentic ethologists, those who instrumentalize other species by experimenting on them or otherwise exploiting them can be expected to be tempted to skepticism about the degree of their thoughts and feelings. A recent narrative of this problem in the early chimpanzee language experiments can be found in Benjamin Hale, "The Last Distinction? Talking to the Animals," *Harper's Magazine* (August 2012), 65-70.

[32] As William Wallace notes, books 21 and 22 of *On Animals* are the heart of Albert's integrative project, where Albert is discussing the hierarchy of perfections among the bodies (and thus minds) of various animals (including humans). See Albertus Magnus,

Now, while those in the "continuity" camp such as Aristotle, Albert, and Aquinas may not have been willing to attribute morality to simians, it would be because while they thought simians shared a variety of emotional and intellectual capacities with human beings, they came to the (empirical) conclusion that simians do not share all the capacities necessary for "reason" or morality.

Moral Blindness

Since the publication of J.M. Coetzee's *The Lives of Animals* and *Elizabeth Costello* almost 20 years ago, there has been a veritable cottage industry of analysis of the significance of his work among philosophers.[33] A central theme that these various philosophers take from Coetzee is the problem of "moral blindness," the question of why and how the vast majority of a society can see a situation (in this case, the institutionalized cruelty of factory farming) as morally insignificant, whereas for a small minority, this situation represents a moral catastrophe, an ongoing situation of moral evil that disconsoles, enrages, and/or paralyzes this minority. While these philosophers vary in their evaluation of the nature and significance of this problem, they all in some way seek to understand the struggle of such persons to maintain their moral identity—in some cases their identity more generally—in a culture they see as so morally foreign, engaged as they see it in morally oppressive and catastrophic practices.

This has long been a concern for moral theology, especially its natural law tradition. It has taken a variety of forms, with some philosophers and theologians (e.g., David Burrell, Herbert Fingerette, Stanley Hauerwas, and Gregg Ten Elshof) working on it as the problem of self-deception in ethics. Others, most notably John Noonan in his work on the development of moral doctrine,[34] have pointed to the complexities and dangers in too blithely passing moral judgments on the moral practices of past societies.

A theological ethology

Those who spend their lives studying the behavior (and thus the

---

On Animals: A Medieval Summa Zoologica, trans. Kenneth F. Kitchell, and Irven Michael Resnick, forward by William Wallace (Baltimore: Johns Hopkins University Press, 1999), xviii-xix.

[33] The list of philosophical luminaries responding to Coetzee's work includes Stanley Cavell, Cora Diamond, Ian Hacking, John McDowell, Peter Singer, and especially Stephen Mulhall. Stanley Hauerwas in "Bearing Reality," his Presidential Address to the Society of Christian Ethics in 2012, also offers a response to themes raised by Coetzee (and Cora Diamond).

[34] See especially John Noonan, *A Church that Can and Cannot Change: The Development of Catholic Moral Teaching* (Notre Dame: University of Notre Dame Press, 2005), especially the final section where Noonan speculates about contemporary moral practices that he believes future generations will be tempted to look back on at us with moral horror and indignation.

nature) of individual animal species diverge in their motives for doing so. Let me give just a few examples. For instance, anthropologists and paleontologists may be interested in primates to gain a better understanding of human prehistory. Agriculturalists may be interested in understanding cows and pigs so they can be raised and slaughtered not only more "humanely," but also more efficiently and effectively (e.g., Temple Grandin). Biological scientists may study rats and dogs to understand the limits of applicability to humans of their experimental results. Zoologists may be interested in understanding the natures of polar bears, pandas, tigers and elephants to design better enclosures at zoos (or circus acts) so the animals are happier and put on a better show for their human visitors. These motives can certainly be all well and good, but they are not in the end, so to speak, about the apes, bears, cows, tigers, and rats themselves. It is still ultimately all about humans. This is what I would call "anthropocentric ethology."

And to the extent it is ultimately about us humans, such studiers of animals have at least a potential conflict of interest. In the same way we do not presume that the advertiser's or the automobile salesperson's quest to "understand us" is so they can better serve our good, we should at least be suspicious about the understanding of a species gained by persons whose end in obtaining that understanding is ultimately not the good of that species. To put it in the extreme: Should we rely on the factory farmer to educate us about cognitive abilities (or ability to suffer) of pigs?

There are, no doubt, anthropocentric ethologists as well as other individuals in the disciplines mentioned above who do in fact study individual species out of the love of understanding a species as an end in itself, or at least have mixed motives. For example, they may be in those disciplines because it allows them to make a living while their true love and interest is an understanding of the nature and good of a particular species. Fair enough.

Furthermore, this is eminently possible, as we constantly rely on persons whose profession (in the traditional sense) is to understand and promote the good of those they serve. We expect our physicians to understand us in order to act in our best interests in healing our bodies (as opposed to selling us a "medical procedure" that we don't need). Similarly, we expect our priests to be seeking to understand us to act on the best interests of our soul (as opposed to seeking an endowment for the parish organ). So too it is eminently reasonable that some people may seek to understand and promote the good of the particular species they study.

And this bring us to theological ethology, which, as I propose above, is the discipline that seeks to understand each species in light of its own authentic natural and supernatural good,[35] understood as flourishing according to its nature.[36] And moral theology, with its interdisciplinary focus and emphasis on the good, and its particular resources to avoid the lure of anthropocentric ethology, is in a particularly good place to serve as a home basis for this field. In fact, a theological ethology may be thought of as analogous to traditional natural law thought on what we can understand about human nature and flourishing *qua* human nature (Jean Porter's work, both in this issue and more generally is exemplary in this regard).

CONCLUSION

As noted previously, for far too long theological discussions about non-human animals have treated them all as one, with no recognition of their particular natures or what we might owe them to allow them to flourish. We can expect a theological ethology to help us understand far more authentically than we have been able to do so far, the true extent of emotional, rational, and moral capacities of a large number of species about which hitherto we have known so little.

As St. Alphonsus is the patron saint of moral theology, it is obvious to propose St. Albert the Great as the patron saint for theological ethology. For while a man of his time and place, a time and place that had infinitely fewer resources to come to an understanding of the great diversity of species with which we share the earth, St. Albert produced his extraordinary *On Animals*, which while certainly outdated in profound ways, nevertheless provides a paradigm for how moral theologians might do theological ethology. Among other virtues, his work exemplifies all the characteristics I have been calling for. Albert clearly recognized humans as one among all the other animals (though a very special one). Albert believed in continuity in the natures of animals, believing that creatures of like bodily natures could be expected to have like mental (and perhaps spiritual) natures. As such Albert (like Aristotle before him and Thomas after him) paved the way for an (at least in theory) unproblematic reception of the insights of (a truly scientific) evolutionary theory. Albert also clearly rejected cognitive parsimony. While an elaboration of this is beyond the scope of this article, Albert's view that humans were the only "rational" and hence "moral" species was, I would argue, a conclusion reached primarily on the basis of empirical understanding of the natures of other animals. In light of the growing consensus in contemporary ethology, I believe that Albert would have had no objections to affirming that—based on

---

35 A discussion of the supernatural good of animal species besides humans is beyond the scope of this article, but a starting place for any theological discussion of the matter would be scriptural sources such as Romans 8.

36 This I take to be the thrust of Charles Camosy and Susan Kopp's paper in this volume.

adequate empirical evidence—other species might well be rational and/or moral.[37]

While it is still probably a little early to be making categorical pronouncements that this or that species can be deemed to be "moral," in say, a Thomistic understanding of ethics, this is quite definitely now a very open question for ethology and philosophy and it most certainly should be for moral theology. And while I may be shown wrong, I fully expect that it is only a matter of time before official Catholic theology comes to recognize at least a form of morality (and for that matter personhood) in at least a few of our fellow species.

While this may open up new avenues of fellowship between humans and other species, I fully expect that for the most part the lives of most animals will remain largely if not utterly a mystery to us. We may hope that this lack of clarity will inspire in us increased humility (rather than presumption). It also perhaps gives us another reason to eagerly anticipate the eschaton.[38] MT

---

[37] For more on this topic, see my "Just Chimpanzees? A Thomistic Perspective on Ethics in a Non-Human Species,"forthcoming in Jonathan K. Crane, ed., *Beastly Morality: Animals as Moral Agents* (New York: Columbia University Press, 2015).

[38] I wish to think Charles Camosy and Celia Deane-Drummond for their helpful comments and criticisms of an earlier draft of this essay.

Journal of Moral Theology, Vol. 3, No. 2 (2014): 35-53

Animals, Evil, and Family Meals

Julie Hanlon Rubio

FOR SOME, THE MORAL IMPERATIVE to avoid meat-eating is obvious. Children who figure out that meat equals animals are often disgusted. They vow to stop eating animals right away. Once they understand, they do not want to participate. They ask the questions adults have forgotten about and look at pictures we cannot bear to see. Yet often they do not get very far into their vegetarianism before giving up. The adults in their lives are still responsible for making food available to them, and most of these adults are not convinced of the duty to avoid meat eating.

Yet, there is no shortage of serious ethical argumentation against eating meat. Ethicists ask, "What are animals? What duties do human persons have toward them? How morally problematic is animal suffering and death? What sort of changes should be adopted by those who see this set of problems?" Two Christian vegetarians explain, "When regarding cooked flesh, meat eaters see food, while vegetarians often see animal and human suffering and death."[1] Many come to believe that we should never eat meat—because animals have certain rights that cannot be violated, because they share important characteristics with humans that suggest a duty of respect or the virtue of kindness, because animals suffer and die needlessly, or because they should be under stewardship rather than dominion.[2] It may be allowed that in some times and places, or in rare cases of particular health issues, individuals may need to eat meat but, today, when alternatives are widely available, there is little justification for meat-eating for most people.

In this essay, I explore a different possibility: the idea that "less meat" is a justifiable ethical stance that respects the dignity of animal life. First, I will describe eating factory-farmed meat as a form of material cooperation with evil that causes undue suffering to animals.

---

[1] Stephen R. Kaufman and Nathan Braun, *Good News for All Creation: Vegetarianism as Christian Stewardship* (Cleveland: Vegetarian Advocates Press, 2002), 44.

[2] Influential arguments for vegetarianism include: Peter Singer, *Animals Liberation: The Definitive Classic of the Movement* (New York: Harper, 2009) and John Robbins, *Diet for a New America*, 25th Anniversary Ed. (New York: New World Library, 2012). On Christian vegetarianism, see Charles C. Camosy, *For Love of Animals: Christian Ethics, Consistent Action* (Cincinnati: Franciscian Media, 2013) and Andrew Linzey, *Christianity and the Rights of Animals* (New York: Crossroads, 1987).

Second, I will locate the practice of eating in its familial, communal, and social contexts in order to argue that while it may not be necessary for health or ideal to eat or serve meat, doing so may sometimes be an important way to realize certain relational and social goods. Third, I will suggest that everyone has an obligation to lessen cooperation with social evil and increase cooperation with social good by avoiding factory-farmed meat. In the conclusion, I recognize the ideal of strict vegetarianism, while allowing for the compromise of flexitarianism in a fallen world where obligations to ourselves, other persons, and animals often conflict.

Between Clear Arguments and Murky Practices

Before moving to my first point, I need to say a word about two assumptions that lead me to explore this line of argumentation. First, it seems that Catholic moral theology is entering a new phase of reflection on animals. Not so long ago, Germain Grisez was able to claim with little qualification that animals, "not being persons, have no rights, and their lives lack the dignity of human life. This is precisely why it can be appropriate deliberately to kill them… to serve any significant human interest… [though they do] have their own special value" and deserve "respect."[3] Today, many question whether this traditional stance is adequate. They ask us to consider animals as beings created by God with their own inherent dignity. They point to capacities for feeling, reasoning, and suffering which may have previously been unknown or overlooked. They suggest that animals deserve more kindness and respect than we currently give them. They push us to consider whether factory-farmed meat (which accounts for almost all meat in the U.S.) can be consumed at all.[4] Though Catholic teaching still certainly allows for meat-eating, new questions are being raised about what sort of meat-eating practice is in keeping with our duty of respect for animals. While acknowledging ongoing controversy about the nature of animals and the claims they have on persons, and without claiming an original position on this subject, I consider some of the practical implications of greater respect for animals.

Second, I am struck by the large number of people I have met who are not vegetarian but do try to avoid factory-farmed meat and eat less meat overall. Though we do not have as much data as we need on the number of vegetarians and less-meat eaters in the U.S., I believe there is enough data to suggest a trend. Only a small percentage of adults in

---

[3] Germain Grisez, *The Way of the Lord Jesus: Vol. III: Difficult Moral Questions* (Quincy: Franciscian, 1997), 420. Grisez rejects Christian arguments for vegetarianism, 423.

[4] John Berkman, "Are We Addicted to the Suffering of Animals? Animal Cruelty and the Catholic Moral Tradition," in *A Faith Embracing All Creatures: Addressing Commonly Asked Questions about Animals*, ed. Tripp York and Andy Alexis-Baker (Eugene: Cascade, 2012).

the U.S., perhaps 3-5%, claim to be vegetarian or vegan.[5] Though it may seem that more people are embracing counter-cultural eating practices, the percentages of vegetarians and vegans have not changed significantly in the last two decades.[6] More-over, a Yale University research team recently found that fewer than .1% of adults are strict vegetarians. That is, the majority of those who say that they "consider themselves" vegetarian eat meat at least sometimes, and new categories are proliferating (e.g., pescatarian, flexitarian, semi-vegetarian, and vegetarians who eat meat only when others serve it).[7] While the animal rights movement can claim some important successes, U.S. meat consumption rose from 178 pounds of red meat and poultry per year in 1978 to 222 pounds per year in 2007 (though beef consumption decreased and chicken consumption increased).[8]

Moreover, one study suggests that three quarters of people who become vegetarian eventually go back to eating meat.[9] Most become vegetarian out of concern for animal welfare and say they return to meat because of health concerns or "hassle."[10] Only a tiny minority change their minds on ethical grounds. They are still concerned about animal welfare, just unable or unwilling to follow through. As most experts agree that, for the vast majority, vegetarianism is a healthy choice, "the hassle" seems to be the most significant reason that people give up abstaining from meat completely.

In the current cultural context, at least in the U.S., it can be very hard to avoid eating meat and choosing not to eat it may sometimes put other values at risk. If you are single and live alone, it might be relatively easy to cook vegetarian meals for yourself, order vegetarian when eating out, and quietly abstain at gatherings of friends who may not eat as you do, but at least view your choices sympathetically.[11] If

---

[5] Frank Newport, "In U.S., 5% Consider Themselves Vegetarians" (July 26, 2012), www.gallup.com/poll/156215/consider-themselves-vegetarians.aspx. Newport found 5% vegetarian and 2% vegan. Studies that use the language "consider yourself" typically find higher numbers than those that ask if people "never eat meat." See also: "Vegetarianism in America," www.vegetariantimes.com/article/-vegetarianism-in-america/ (3.2% vegetarian); Charles Stahler, "How Often do Americans Eat Vegetarian Meals?" (May 12, 2012), www.vrg.org/blog/2012/05/18/-how-often-do-americans-eat-vegetarian-meals-and-how-many-adults-in-the-u-s-are-vegetarian/ (4% vegetarian); Ashley Palmer, "2011 Vegetarian and Vegan Stats," PETA, www.peta.org/living/food/2011-vegetarian-vegan-stats/ (5% vegetarian).

[6] Newport, "5% Consider Themselves Vegetarians."

[7] Newport, "5% Consider Themselves Vegetarians."

[8] Newport, "5% Consider Themselves Vegetarians."

[9] Hal Herzog, "Why Do Most Vegetarians Go Back to Eating Meat?" *Psychology Today* (June 20, 2011), www.psychologytoday.com/blog/animals-and-us/201106/-why-do-most-vegetarians-go-back-eating-meat. Herzog finds 1-3% vegetarian.

[10] Herzog, "Why Do Most Vegetarians Go Back to Eating Meat?"

[11] Unmarried adults are twice as likely to be vegetarian. See Hal Herzog, "Why Are There So Few Vegetarians?" *Psychology Today* (Sept 6, 2011), www.psycho-logytoday.com/blog/animals-and-us/201109/why-are-there-so-few-vegetarians.

you are dating or married to a meat eater, things might be a bit more complicated. If you cook for a family with children, host holiday gatherings for relatives, contribute food for church and school social functions, entertain your children's friends, and host neighborhood parties, things become much more complicated. Concern for animal welfare constantly conflicts with duties of hospitality.

However, the ethical movement to change eating habits in a cultural context in which meat is central is not doomed to failure. In the last several years, the drop in meat and poultry consumption has been significant enough to worry meat producers.[12] In fact, "for the first time on record, U.S. per-capita meat consumption has declined for four consecutive years, according to the most recent figures from the U.S. Department of Agriculture. The six percent drop between 2006 and 2010 is the largest sustained decline since recordkeeping began in 1970."[13] Some of the recent drop can be attributed to the recession, but much of it is due to a broader acceptance of "flexitarian" and "less meat" lifestyles as well as cultural movements such as "Meatless Mondays." Thirty-nine percent of those who took part in a recent survey claim to have reduced their meat intake in the last year.[14] Flexitarians, who eat less meat, cite multiple concerns: health, cost, the environment, and animal welfare, and they are on the rise.[15] In a meat-centric culture, this is significant change.

It is in this context of ongoing reflection on what the inherent dignity of animals demands of us and evolution toward flexitarian eating patterns that I attempt to develop an argument that Christians ought to avoid factory-farmed meat but may serve or eat it if avoiding meat or buying cruelty-free meat conflicts with other important obligations.

Eating Meat as Material Cooperation with Evil

Is eating meat morally wrong? Traditionally, Catholic thought has allowed for human use of animals because animals were understood to be lower in the order of creation. Eating meat was not evil but right use. Thomas Aquinas held that animals were different from humans

---

[12] CME Group, *Daily Livestock Report* 9.24 (December 20, 2011), www.daily-livestockreport.com/documents/dlr%2012-20-2011.pdf.

[13] Karen Flynn, "Americans Eating Less Meat, Even as Rest of World Eats More" *Researchscape* (May 8, 2013), www.researchscape.com/health/meat-consumption-trends. See also, Brad Tuttle, "The Meatless (and less meat) Revolution," *Time* (March 22, 2012), http://business.time.com/2012/03/22/the-meatless-and-less-meat-revolution/, and Janet Larsen, "Peak Meat: U.S. Meat Consumption Falling," *Earth Policy Institute* (March 7, 2012), www.earth-policy.org/data_highlights/2012/highlights25.

[14] Flynn, "Americans Eating Less Meat." Still, U.S. consumption is three times the global average.

[15] Eliza Barclay, "Why There's Less Red Meat on Many American Plates," *National Public Radio* (June 27, 2012), www.npr.org/blogs/thesalt/2012/06/27/155837575/why-theres-less-red-meat-served-on-many-american-plates.

and women were different from men, and he therefore assigned to both a place in keeping with their nature. Aquinas, who seems not to have fully grasped the reality of women's nature, might also have been unable to see that animals may have their own "ontological distinctiveness."[16] His influence on the Catholic tradition was considerable. In the manuals that dominated Catholic moral thought from the 18th to the 20th centuries, because animals were considered "brute beasts," not persons, they had no rights, and humans had "no duties of charity or duties of any kind" toward them.[17] Animals were "as things in our regard."[18]

However, there is also a long history of Christian opposition to causing pain to animals if their suffering is not necessary. According to James Gaffney, in the manuals, "cruelty occurs whenever avoidable pain is inflicted for reasons that are disproportionate or indifferent to the interests of the sufferer."[19] The manualists generally had in mind situations in which cruelty was inflicted not "in sport" but "for sport," or for cruelty's sake.[20] Still, contemporary Catholics who work within Thomas' system bring more informed understandings of animals. Charles Camosy asks whether we can begin to look beyond person/non-person binaries to a hierarchy of beings that recognizes the value of non-persons and persons, which "does not mean that, in each and every circumstance, any good of a person necessarily trumps any good of a non-person" but may mean that the good of saving money by eating cheap meat from factory farms may not trump "the more valuable good of chickens not being tortured in such farms."[21] While hierarchy is associated with significant problems with regard to animals in the tradition, "it just seems undeniable that some creatures mirror their creator more perfectly than do others."[22]

Granting human difference from animals in a hierarchical schema allows us to see that even though some animals eat other animals, humans "are a different kind of animal—one which has the power to reflect on our source of ultimate concern and the values associated with it, and then act accordingly."[23] Because we are different, we have more

---

[16] Dorothy Yamamoto, "Aquinas and Animals: Patrolling the Boundary?" in *Animals on the Agenda,* ed. Andrew Linzey and Dorothy Yamamoto (Chicago: University of Illinois Press, 1998), 84. Yamamoto is commenting on Aquinas, *Summa Theologiae,* I q. 64, a. 4.

[17] James Gaffney, "Can Catholic Morality Make Room for Animals?" in *Animals on the Agenda*, 100.

[18] Gaffney, "Can Catholic Morality Make Room," 101.

[19] Gaffney, "Can Catholic Morality Make Room," 105.

[20] Gaffney, "Can Catholic Morality Make Room," 103.

[21] Charles C. Camosy, "Other Animals as Persons? – A Roman Catholic Inquiry," in *Animals as Religious Subjects,* ed. Celia Deane-Drummond and David Clough (Cambridge: T&T Clark, 2013), 273.

[22] Camosy, "Other Animals as Persons?"

[23] Camosy, "Other Animals as Persons?"

responsibility to act with kindness and diminish suffering, even if we believe that all animals and humans are not created equal.

But what does it mean to treat animals with kindness? When is their suffering and death needless? Some argue that all meat-eating is immoral because the preferences of human persons should not outweigh the lives of animals.[24] My intention here is to take up a narrower, more practical question. Assuming that meat-eating is not always sinful, can eating and serving the sort of meat that most people eat (e.g., meat from factory farms) be reconciled with a duty to treat animals with kindness and avoid causing them to suffer needlessly?[25] Descriptions of what happens at factory farms are widely available, so rather than repeating them here, I will assume that familiarity with the reality of meat production would strike most readers as unkind.[26]

Because most people do not personally cause suffering to the animals they eat, the actions in question are the serving and eating of meat that others have procured. What kind of action is this? John Berkman argues that because all factory-farmed meat is "cruelty meat," eating it can be described as "supporting an industry that institutionalizes cruelty."[27] In the Catholic tradition, aiding another in wrongdoing is called "cooperation with evil" though, depending on the circumstances, it can be morally permissible.[28] Formal cooperation, in which one shares the intention of the evildoer, is never permissible. However, material cooperation, when one acts "under duress and does not intend [the evil committed]," can be licit.[29] Berkman contends that eating factory-farmed meat constitutes formal cooperation with evil and is thus morally impermissible.[30] In this case, "cruelty is not a mere evil side-effect or by-product" but "an essential and necessary part of the logic of factory farming." He uses the analogy of buying stolen property. In both cases, you "consent and perhaps contribute to the wrong done to victims of cruelty" and "support and sustain the wrong done

---

[24] See, e.g., Andrew Tardiff, "A Catholic Case for Vegetarianism," *Faith and Philosophy* 15.2 (1998), which argues that unless animals are needed for survival, it is immoral to kill them for food, 220.

[25] Most studies put the percentage of meat coming from factory farms at 95-99%. Unless meat carries a label indicating certification by an external agency (e.g., "animal welfare approved," "certified humane," "organic"), the assumption should be that it comes from factory farms. "Factory Farming," *Farming Forward*, www.farmforward.com/farming-forward/factory-farming. The National Resources Defense Council provides a helpful guide, "The Omnivore's Green Grill," www.nrdc.org/living/eatingwell/grilling-guide/labels.asp.

[26] See, e.g., Peter Singer and Jim Mason, *Ethics of What We Eat* (Emmaus, PA: Rodale, 2007).

[27] Berkman, "Are We Addicted to the Suffering of Animals?," 135.

[28] Cathleen Kaveny, *Law's Virtues: Fostering Autonomy and Solidarity in American Society* (Washington, DC: Georgetown, 2012), 246-48.

[29] Gerald Magill, "A Moral Compass for Wrongdoing," *Voting and Holiness,* ed. Nicholas P. Cafardi (New York: Paulist, 2012), 135-57.

[30] Berkman, "Are We Addicted to the Suffering of Animals?," 135.

by [the system]."[31] In cases of material cooperation with evil, the harm done to victims is non-essential, indirect, and consensual, and claims of duress may prevail. However, in the case of meat, the evil is essential to the system, the animals do not consent to it, and the harm is unavoidable. There is no need that would justify it, nor is there duress to excuse it. Only "ignorance, laziness, or gluttony" can explain our continued meat eating.[32]

But is this the only way to describe the action in question? According to Charles Curran, the material cooperator with evil does not share the intentions of the actor engaged in the evil action, is engaged in a neutral or good action, and achieves a good via cooperation that outweighs the harm of the evil.[33] Kaveny concurs, saying the actor who "foresees but does not intend that his or her action will facilitate the wrongful action of the primary agent" engages in material cooperation, not formal.[34] Both authors emphasize intention as the key factor differentiating formal from material cooperation. Building on this understanding, one could argue that since typical meat-eaters do not share the intention of farmers who provide their meat and see themselves engaged in the good action of buying food to feed their families, their cooperation is material.

Nonetheless, meat eaters benefit from the moral evil of factory farming in that their meat is cheaper and more convenient to obtain than meat purchased from alternative sources. With their money, they contribute to wrong-doing. Can this really be licit? If, in a Thomistic framework, "it would not be reasonable to allow a grave evil for a relatively insignificant good," meat-eating can be seen as "a question of destroying goods unnecessarily in the process of securing a good effect," similar to killing a person in self-defense if you could run away.[35] According to this logic, eating meat is not strictly necessary and the good of pleasure does not outweigh the evil inflicted upon animals. In its strongest form, the Thomistic argument for vegetarianism would be, "whenever a person can serve his ends by killing plants instead of animals, then he may not kill animals since, as ontically superior to plants, doing so in those circumstances would constitute more than necessary violence" and would be "out of proportion to the end."[36] In the more limited context of this essay, the unnecessary animal suffering inflicted in factory farming seems disproportionate to the good of enjoying food. It does not seem a stretch to consider what

---

[31] Berkman, "Are We Addicted to the Suffering of Animals?," 135.

[32] Berkman, "Are We Addicted to the Suffering of Animals?," 136.

[33] Charles E. Curran, *A History of Moral Theology in the U.S.* (Washington, DC: Georgetown, 2008), 56.

[34] Kaveny, *Law's Virtues*, 248.

[35] Tardiff, "A Catholic Case for Vegetarianism," 212.

[36] Tardiff, "A Catholic Case for Vegetarianism," 213.

is done to animals on factory farms evil.[37] Thus it seems that the meat-eating person must be cooperating with evil in an illicit way.

Yet, if one reviews the cases analyzed in the moral manuals, the act of eating factory-farmed meat seems to fit the framework of licit material cooperation. This is especially true if we limit our focus to cases involving cooperation in business or the workplace. In the classic case of printed materials "inimical to faith or morals," manualist Heribert Jone judges most of those who directly contribute to the process to be engaging in material cooperation because they do not share the intentions of the author.

Although Jone does not specify how the printed materials go against faith or morals, the example is similar to others in which the Catholic faith was thought to be somehow undermined, such as renting a hall for an "immoral show," or providing supplies or labor for a non-Catholic place of worship. Proximate cooperation is only permissible for a grave reason, such as the need of a job, but less proximate cooperative actions could be justifiable for a moderately grave reason. The more remote and unnecessary the cooperation of a particular person, the easier it was to justify for relatively minor reasons.[38] When manualists such as Jone looked at the morality of purchasing or otherwise financially or practically contributing to evil, they were most often talking about material cooperation with evil.

However, we have to ask if eating factory-farmed meat is a totally different kind of act. Perhaps, as in the case of stolen property, "if I eat factory-farmed bacon or ribs, I consent and perhaps contribute to the wrong done to the victims of the cruelty, and I support and sustain the wrong done by the factory farm industry. Hence I formally cooperate in the cruelty to pigs when I buy and/or eat the bacon or ribs."[39]

Yet in Jone's case reviewed above, animosity to Christian faith and morals is certainly central to the literature being produced, yet almost all of the many ways of contributing to the production and profitability of illicit literature are judged to be potentially permissible acts of material cooperation. The willingness of manualists to excuse material cooperation with evil actions is sometimes striking, for instance, in the case of the nurse who assists a surgeon with an illicit operation, the servant who brings letters or gifts to his master's lover, and taxi driver

---

[37] Robert N. Wennberg, *God, Humans, and Animals: An Invitation to Enlarge Our Moral Universe* (Grand Rapids: Eerdmans, 2003), 235-9.

[38] Heribert Jone, *Moral Theology*, trans. Urban Adelman (Westminster: Newman, 1945), 92-98. The manuals are shaped by their context, in which sexual sins received harsh treatment and social sin was all but ignored. The bias against non-Catholics and the harsh judgment of the media and arts make the cases difficult for the modern reader. Moreover, the manualists themselves did not always agree on what sorts of material cooperation were licit, see Grisez, *Difficult Moral Questions*, Appendix II, 890.

[39] Berkman, "Are We Addicted to the Suffering of Animals?," 135.

who takes customers to "houses of ill-repute."[40] Moreover, the more remote the cooperation, the more likely they were to label it licit.[41] The manualists seem to assume that contact with evil is unavoidable, duties often conflict, and people have limited power to change all situations to which they rightfully object.

Some might argue, following Grisez's understanding of cooperation, that a meat-eater would "prefer" an alternate way of producing meat but nonetheless accepts the process as it is. Thus she still has a "bad will" and engages in formal cooperation.[42] Yet it is crucial to take account of the context of the imperfect world in which we are constantly faced with imperfect choices. "Because of the reality of sin in the world," Gerald Magill writes, "good and evil are intertwined."[43] Once we become conscious of all of the "good-intertwined-with-evil" involved in so many of our purchases and lifestyle choices, the potential to cooperate with evil seems limitless. To claim that we accept and intend all of the evil to which we contribute our votes, money, time, and action seems to assign too much moral responsibility to limited human beings. Material cooperation seems a better term to describe our reluctant, yet morally flawed choices.

Eating in Context:
Permissible Material Cooperation of Meat Eating

Simply labeling an action as material does not let cooperators off the hook. For material cooperation to be permissible, it has to meet certain conditions. The less proximate, less essential to the evil action, and the more necessary to my good or neutral action, the more likely it is to be licit.[44] Also, the gravity of the evil in question and any duress an actor might be under must be considered.[45] In the moral manuals, "many (although not all) of the cases involve workers struggling to reconcile their consciences with the demands of the workplace.... [O]n the one hand, losing a job meant losing a livelihood and the abil-

---

[40] See, e.g., Henry Davis, *Moral and Pastoral Theology,* Vol. I: *Human Acts, Law, Sin, Virtue* (London: Sheed & Ward, 1945), 347-52. Still, the manuals had serious limits; see James F. Keenan, "Moral Horizons in Healthcare: Reproductive Technologies and Catholic Identity," in *Infertility: A Crossroad of Faith, Medicine, and Technology*, ed. Kevin Wm. Wildes (Boston: Kluwer, 1997): 53-71.

[41] Grisez, *Difficult Moral Questions*, Appendix II, suggests that reconsideration of the import of proximity is needed, 890. I agree but hold that when we begin to name remote material cooperation with evil, because of the nearly limitless ways in which we cooperate, the principle should function only as a tool for discernment and growth in virtue.

[42] Grisez, *Difficult Moral Questions*, 892.

[43] Magill, "A Moral Compass," 138.

[44] Kaveny, *Law's Virtues*, 248.

[45] Kaveny, *Law's Virtues*, 250.

ity to fulfill family obligations while, on the other, committing a mortal sin risked the loss of eternal happiness."[46] Kaveny notes that the framework is really not set up to deal with problems of social evil to which many actors contribute from afar and from which many actors benefit.[47] Nonetheless, I have argued elsewhere that the principle of moral cooperation can be adapted for use in social ethics as long we use it as a tool for discernment rather than a way to identify with precision sin and culpability.[48] Thus the exercise we engage in here is an attempt to adapt an instrument used by manualists to aid priests in the confessional in their work of handing out penances to the much murkier terrain of social ethics.

To determine if an action involving cooperation is licit, we first have to describe it well. Eating is an inherently social action.[49] People buy food for households, eat meals together, and often socialize over food and drinks.[50] Eating plays a crucial role in sustaining culture because families and communities gather over food not just at mealtimes, but at weddings, funerals, birthdays, graduations, and other important ritual moments both religious and secular.

Women are more often those charged with sustaining relationships, families, and cultures through food. For her book, *Feeding the Family*, sociologist Marjorie Devault interviewed women to better understand how they viewed the work of food provision. The women emphasized that meals were "organizer(s) of family life," events where they performed their identity as a family.[51] Even today, "feeding remains a central ritual… in the production of family life itself."[52] Meals are still "social events that bring family members together… provide a basis for establishing and maintaining family culture, and… create a mutual recognition of the family as a group."[53] The work of producing a meal includes planning, shopping, cooking and serving family members, and this is why, the women told Devault, "the food provided cannot be just any food, but must be… food their families liked."[54] Women organize meals around the preferences of others for the sake of the

---

[46] Kaveny, *Law's Virtues*, 247.
[47] M. Cathleen Kaveny, "Appropriation of Evil: Cooperation's Mirror Image," *Theological Studies* 61.2 (2000): 280-313.
[48] Julie Hanlon Rubio, "Moral Cooperation with Evil and Social Ethics," *Journal of the Society of Christian Ethics*, 31.1 (2011): 103-22.
[49] Marjorie L. DeVault, *Feeding the Family: The Social Organization of Caring as Gendered Work* (Chicago: University of Chicago Press, 1991), 35.
[50] Julie Hanlon Rubio, "Toward a Just Way of Eating," in *Green Discipleship: Catholic Theological Ethics and the Environment*, ed. Tobias Winright (Winona: Anselm, 2011), 366-68.
[51] Devault, *Feeding the Family*, 38.
[52] Devault, *Feeding the Family*, 38.
[53] Devault, *Feeding the Family*, 39.
[54] Devault, *Feeding the Family*, 40.

common life of their families. In their eyes, "responding to these individual preferences is not a personal favor, but a requirement of the work. Family members may not eat if they don't like what is served."[55] The women in Devault's study were especially concerned to serve foods their children would eat, and "were scrupulously careful not to give their own preferences any special weight."[56] They understood feeding not simply as meeting individuals' needs for sustenance but as "a way of caring for others well."[57]

Caring work is not limited to the immediate family. Rather, women are also often responsible for "kinwork," which includes "the organization of holiday gatherings" and "the creation and maintenance of quasi-kin relations."[58] The maintenance of kinship ties across households is viewed by many women as crucial work, and they worry "about their failures to keep families close through constant contact and about their failures to create perfect holiday celebrations."[59] The needs of children and the elderly are especially salient. These activities of kinwork are labors of love but, like preparing family meals, they are also a form of work.[60] Food is central to extended family gatherings, and thus choices about what to serve are part of the work. Those doing caring work must balance multiple values: strengthening family, passing on traditions, keeping costs low, cooking people's favorites, and balancing the many different tastes and ethical concerns of people joined in kin networks.

All of this complicates the typical argument for avoiding factory-farmed meat. A person's choice about what to eat is not simply an individual choice because eating is a social practice embedded in families, communities, and cultures. The ethical question is not only about whether to consume certain foods oneself, but also about what to buy, cook, serve, and contribute to social gatherings. In this context, the intention of a flexitarian is to share meals with people she loves, serve foods they enjoy, and sustain family and kin ties.[61] In no way does she desire, need, or approve of the evil of factory farming. She cannot fairly be described as "ignorant, lazy, or gluttonous." Rather, like the

---

[55] Devault, *Feeding the Family*, 40.

[56] Devault, *Feeding the Family*, 43.

[57] Devault, *Feeding the Family*, 87.

[58] Micaela Di Leonardo, "The Female World of Cards and Holidays: Women, Families, and the Work of Kinship," in *Rethinking the Family: Some Feminist Questions*, Rev. Ed., ed. Barrie Thorne with Marilyn Yalom (Boston: Northeastern University Press, 1992), 248.

[59] Di Leonardo, "The Female World of Cards and Holidays," 251.

[60] Di Leonardo, "The Female World of Cards and Holidays," 258.

[61] I employ female pronouns here to highlight two things: (1) the reality that women still do more feeding work than men and (2) the fact that the manuals often assume a male worker whose vocational duty is to provide, and rarely consider other vocational duties of parents. Of course, both men and women have both kinds of duties and may experience these duties as a kind of duress.

taxi driver taking customers to the brothel or the printer of the program of the illicit show, she is under some duress in view of her vocation which includes serving food in social contexts, and, given fundamental commitments to family and kin, she does the best she can.

One might hold that other options are available. The flexitarian can avoid cooking meat dishes or pay more for cruelty-free meat. Certainly, it is not wrong to expect some efforts to cook vegetarian meals involving beans, cheese, lentils, eggs, and soy products. Someone who claims concern for animal welfare and reluctant cooperation with factory farming must try to find substitutes for meat, cook appetizing meat-less meals, and inform others about why these choices are important to her. Families should also make efforts to buy meat not produced by factory farms. Not all families can afford to spend two or three times as much on meat, and their responsibilities for avoiding cooperation will vary with income. It is also harder in some families or communities than others to introduce vegetarian dishes or make the sacrifices necessary to afford ethical meat while preparing meals that are truly welcoming for all.

Does this description excuse wrongdoing? Is a more rigorous understanding of sin required in a Catholic context? Interesting enough, though the moral manuals are sometimes associated with overzealousness with regard to sin, they often describe ordinary actions in just this way. Though flawed in their focus on individual sin and their failure to attend to injustice, the manuals offer a framework in which individual actions matter and awareness of cooperation with evil is crucial to the moral life. However, the questions offered to confessors to help people discern when cooperation crosses the line are indicative of some practical realism. The manuals managed to generate an ethic for imperfect human beings with multiple commitments because they made "the assumption that individuals are constrained by the circumstances of their lives" and held that duties to avoid evil are stronger "the more the duties of our state of life or of our vocation command us to prevent such evil effects."[62] When one's vocation involves planning meals, buying food, and serving other people, one's ability to avoid evil is constrained. Respect for animals can conflict with respect for family and friends. In cases like these, prudential judgment is required to discern rightly one's duties. At times, it seems that serving and eating meat may constitute a necessary and permissible form of material cooperation with evil.

Social Virtue, Corporate Vice, and Cooperation with Good

Because the moral manuals of the 19th and 20th century were written for confessors, they are much more concerned with determining

---

[62] Rubio, "Moral Cooperation," 106.

the sinfulness of particular actions than describing the good life. They are much better at defining vice than inspiring virtue. Moral theologians with different perspectives tend to agree that while the manualists encouraged pastoral sensitivity, they rarely attempted to describe the shape of excellence or holiness in positive terms.[63] However, the Second Vatican Council called for a renewal of Catholic moral theology, and interest in virtue and growth soon followed. Consequently, obligations to avoid even permissible material cooperation and strive for virtue can be more fully considered.

The implications of a virtue approach seem clear for those who are eating alone or with others who share concerns about animal welfare. Avoiding factory-farmed meat in these situations seems obligatory. When serving food to others with different views, the issues become more complicated and buying or serving factory-farmed meat might be permissible when important to one's primary obligations to family and community. Eating meat as a guest when it is served in someone else's home may be obligatory if one's host would otherwise be deeply offended. Yet in the manuals, because social structures were assumed rather than analyzed, moral reflection tended to focus on the question of whether or not an activity was permissible.[64] Today we should strive to recognize structural sin and discern obligations to challenge it.[65]

One might claim that because social sin is so pervasive, we cannot possibly consider ourselves implicated by all of the many ways we contribute to it. Yet, the Catholic tradition holds that we can sin both in action and inaction.[66] Dorothy Day drew attention to complicity with the government, saying, "Whatever you buy is taxed, so that you are, in effect, helping to support the state's preparation for war exactly to the extent of your attachment to worldly things."[67] Peter Singer's famous story of the person who fails to save the drowning toddler lest she ruin her shoes implies that each time we buy something unnecessary, we choose pleasure over the lives of starving people.[68] As Camosy points out, this is simply a riff on the story of the Good Samaritan.[69] If we take these charges seriously, most of us materially

---

[63] See, e.g., Charles E. Curran, *Origins of Moral Theology in the United States: Three Different Approaches* (Washington, DC: Georgetown University Press, 1997), 278, and John S. Grabowski, *Sex and Virtue: An Introduction to Sexual Ethics* (Washington, DC: Georgetown University Press, 2003), 17-18.

[64] Curran, *Origins of Moral Theology,* 159

[65] Grisez, *Difficult Moral Questions*, Appendix II, 879-83, raises important questions about cases of material cooperation the manualists might have excused.

[66] Charles C. Camosy, *Peter Singer and Christian Ethics: Beyond Polarization* (New York: Cambridge University, 2012), 144.

[67] Dorothy Day, "Little by Little," *Dorothy Day, Selected Writings*, ed. Robert Ellsberg (Maryknoll, NY: Orbis, 1998), 111.

[68] Peter Singer, *The Life You Can Save* (New York: Random House, 2009), 3.

[69] Camosy, *Peter Singer and Christian Ethics*, 142.

cooperate with evil by buying things that are taxed, buying things we do not need, and failing to contribute enough to charity. If virtuous persons help those who are hurting and strive to ensure that their money does not contribute to violence, there is some vice in all contrary actions.

Even if one disagrees with Day's assessment of taxes or war or thinks Singer asks too much, most realize that in a globalized world, we routinely buy things made in factories where human dignity is denied. The vast majority of our clothing is made in sweatshops where living wages and fair working conditions remain a distant dream. Though some argue that companies are working on improving conditions, the collapse of a factory in Bangladesh in 2013 that killed over 800 people brought to light once again the utter misery of life in these factories, the lack of oversight, and the unwillingness of Western companies and customers to take responsibility.[70] And yet we continue to buy new clothing. As with meat, few of us "need" a new sweater when thrift stores make buying used so easy. We could make due with used, learn to sew, or pay more for fair trade. We could organize large campaigns to pressure companies to change, and make do with fewer clothes until they did.[71] Yet, through our personal choices and our failures to act, we reject these options and instead cooperate with social vice.

One might argue that actions such as paying taxes, buying sweatshop clothing, or eating factory-farmed meat are insignificant compared to other forms of remote cooperation with evil, because the actions of one buyer are not necessary for the evil in question to continue, but viewed differently they can seem more serious, because the actions of many "have a significant effect on the practices they facilitate."[72] Kaveny uses the concept of "aggregated agency" to describe shared responsibility for collective actions. Catholic moral theology has not traditionally paid much attention to these sorts of actions, yet it is through them that most of us have our most significant impacts on structures of sin.

Kaveny sees that two kinds of responses are necessary: personal and political. First, we should acknowledge that engaging in wrongdoing, however remote, stains our character and that of those around us, so discernment about obligations to reduce wrongdoing is necessary. We should become better informed about how our daily activities

---

[70] See Jason Burke, "Bangladesh Factory Fires: Fashion Industry's Latest Crisis," *The Guardian*, Dec. 8, 2013, www.theguardian.com/world/2013/dec/08/bangladesh-factory-fires-fashion-latest-crisis.

[71] Boycotts may not help but consumer pressure has led to some changes. See, Vikas Bajaj, "Before You Buy That Tee Shirt," *New York Times* (May 18, 2013), www.nytimes.com/2013/05/19/opinion/sunday/before-you-buy-that-tshirt.html?src=recpb&_r=1&.

[72] Kaveny, *Law's Virtues*, 262.

"are enabled by broad patterns of collective wrongdoing," think about how best to "express solidarity with persons harmed by those evils," consider if it might be possible to engage in a "countervailing action… to offset complicity" such as "donating to an organization that combats child labor."[73] Along with working at the personal level, we should also ask how best we might work for social change. Kaveny suggests that boycotts, while sometimes important, are not always effective, nor are they the only means of bringing about the reforms we desire.[74] Positive political engagement may sometimes be the smarter way to cooperate with good.

Kaveny's framework for responding to forms of cooperation with evil involving aggregated agency assumes an understanding of solidarity as the virtue that we use to respond to social sin. In contemporary Catholic Social Teaching, solidarity is central, though we acknowledge that the concept has been expressed differently in different eras.[75] Solidarity is both a personal and a social virtue that calls for "change of heart as well as change of structures."[76]

What might this mean for those struggling not simply to free themselves from cooperation with factory farming but also to change the social structures which make harm to animals normative? I have already established that, at the personal level, respect for animals should lead individuals to avoid factory-farmed meat. Doing so will require becoming better informed, because it is currently difficult to determine which companies actually prioritize ethical treatment of animals and which labels can be trusted. Because ethically-sourced meat is expensive, those in charge of shopping for households will have to work at adjusting their food budgets, redirecting money away expensive prepared and junk foods to ethically-sourced meat, meat substitutes, and plant-based foods. They will need to seek out new recipes, learn to think differently about meals and parties, and adapt their tastes.[77] This will all take time.

But the changes of individuals and households alone will not change the system. Those convinced of the evils of factory farming might also express solidarity in support for organizations fighting for better conditions for animals. Awareness of hormones and antibiotics in meat is growing, and as people recognize the health dangers, they are beginning to see connections between the health and welfare of human persons and animals. It is becoming easier to find organic meat

73 Kaveny, *Law's Virtues*, 263.

74 Kaveny, *Law's Virtues*, 263.

75 Charles E. Curran, Kenneth R. Himes, O.F.M., and Thomas A. Shannon, "Commentary on *Sollicitudo Rei Socialis*," *Modern Catholic Social Teaching: Commentaries and Interpretations,* ed. Kenneth R. Himes, O.F.M. (Washington, DC: Georgetown University Press, 2005), 429.

76 Curran, Himes, and Shannon, "Commentary on *Sollicitudo Rei Socialis*," 430.

77 Rubio, "Toward a Just Way of Eating," 366-68, 370-76.

and meat labeled hormone-free, antibiotic free, or GMO free, because health concerns have increased demand for these products, and producers know customers are willing to pay more for them. However, factory-farmed products still dominate the market. Celia Deane-Drummond argues that we need to "affirm a theology of creation that recognizes humanity as integrated with the material, created world."[78] Successful political campaigns will make these connections in order convince people of "the importance of viewing humanity not as distant from the creaturely world, but existing in mutual relationship" with animals and all of creation.[79]

Between the personal and political is the realm of community or what Catholic Social Teaching has traditionally called "intermediary associations." Though long affirmed as central to Catholic social thought, this sphere remains a footnote in most of social ethics.[80] Here, there is plenty of work to be done. While sometimes, one may choose to serve or eat meat that is served without knowing its origins, it is also necessary to work at changing the social structures that make meat-eating so pervasive and vegetarianism so difficult to maintain. The Meatless Monday campaign is a great way to re-shape culture one step at a time.[81] Families can also begin changing the shape of social gatherings by: serving less meat (e.g., tacos instead of barbeque), bringing popular vegetarian dishes to potlucks (e.g., humus and vegetables), offering vegetarian alternatives at gatherings hosted at their homes, and suggesting restaurants with many vegetarian options for gatherings of friends. Slowly, "by little and by little," they can begin to change the social structures that lead to such pervasive material cooperation with evil.[82]

Solidarity is a virtue oriented not just to human persons but also to animals with whom we share the earth, especially because they are vulnerable. It should lead us to aim for consuming with compassion as much as we are able while taking account of conflicting goods, to work for political change, and to re-shape communities by introducing alternatives to factory-farmed meat into the social contexts in which so much eating takes place. Through reducing their own cooperation with evil and working to change sinful social structures by cooperating with good from the top down and the bottom up, as well as in the space between, Christians can treat social sin as it ought to be treated, not

---

[78] Celia Deane Drummond, "Animal Ethics: Where Do We Go from here?" in *Moral Theology for the 21st Century: Essays in Celebration of Kevin T. Kelly,* ed. Bernard Hoose, Julie Clague, and Gerald Mannion (New York: T&T Clark, 2008), 159.

[79] Drummond, "Animal Ethics: Where Do We Go from here?," 160.

[80] Julie Hanlon Rubio, *Family Ethics: Practices for Christians* (Washington, DC: Georgetown University Press, 2010), 37-65.

[81] See, www.meatlessmonday.com/.

[82] My virtue approach here is similar to that of John Berkman, "Prophetically Pro-Life," *Josephinum* 6.1 (1998): 52-4.

only as evil from which to extricate themselves but also as evil they seek to end.

Is a Virtue-Based Response to Evil Adequate? Compromise in a Complex World

I have proposed a virtue-based response to what I have identified as the social sin of factory farming. While affirming that we materially cooperate with evil when eating factory farmed meat, I leave room for such cooperation in situations in which one's obligations to family and friends should take precedence, while encouraging local and political practices of solidarity with animals. I imagine that many vegetarians, along with those who always avoid factory-farmed meat, may be growing impatient. After all, I have agreed that what is done to most animals we eat for meat is evil and have allowed that those who partake of it are justly called "cooperators" who benefit from and contribute, through aggregated agency, to the maintenance of social sin. I have viewed the videos and pictures revealing the horrors of factory farming, and I share the revulsion of many vegetarians. If factory farming is truly evil, why allow cooperation with it?

In a recent article, Stephen Bush suggests that when evil arouses moral disgust, we should take it very seriously.[83] Disgust is certainly what motivates many pure vegetarians. Once aware of the processes, they simply cannot imagine eating animal flesh. Bush considers an alternative view that moral horror is often a response to badness, but does not necessarily tell us that something is wrong. Rather, we should understand that, "horrible actions are often wrong actions and that moral horror is an important response to horrifically wrong actions, but not all horrible actions are wrong."[84] Bush disagrees. Horror and revulsion are recognitions of a violation of something sacred. While emotions are not always the best guide to moral reasoning, and we can be critical of them, "we ought not feel horror toward actions we think are morally permissible."[85] The keys to moral horror are intentions and consequences, which rule out things like surgery and just killing, which may arouse visceral feelings of horror.[86] However, "a serious and direct attack on a person" properly elicits moral disgust and calls for nonparticipation.[87]

There is something to this argument. We should take feelings of moral disgust or horror seriously and think about what sort of violation is going on when we have them. Too often, we fail to see evil. More often, we turn away from evil we know is there, telling ourselves that

---

[83] Stephen S. Bush, "Horribly Wrong: Moral Disgust and Killing," *Journal of Religious Ethics* 41.4 (2013): 585-600.
[84] Bush, "Horribly Wrong," 588.
[85] Bush, "Horribly Wrong," 589.
[86] Bush, "Horribly Wrong," 592.
[87] Bush, "Horribly Wrong," 598.

we simply "can't go there" because we cannot face the implications of our connectedness to violation. Bush is right to push for wrestling with emotions that are sometimes important moral guides. To push these feelings aside is to persist in vincible ignorance.[88]

In my view, advocates of Christian vegetarianism, like pacifists, properly lay claim to the moral ideal. If, "God's intention for the world is for all creatures to exist in relationship with each other, not in isolation or competition," killing and eating animals seems at odds with God's work of salvation.[89] Regardless of how much concern for animal welfare is taken into account, the raising of animals for food seems to bear at least some marks of violence and thus to point away from what God desires for creation.

The problem, it seems to me, is that the evils of the poverty we neglect to alleviate with our excess money and the wars we fail to protest but support with our tax dollars, are evil, too, and even more so because they involve violations of human persons. We should feel horror in the faces of those evils, too. We simply cannot extract ourselves from everything that legitimately inspires horror in us. There is no evil-free zone. The tragedy of human existence does not allow for a clean conscience. Instead, we have to be content with our always partial efforts to do less evil and more good.

In the case of meat-eating, though the choice seems simple when considered from an individual perspective, when placed in the context of family and community it is far more complex. The moral manuals allowed for some material cooperation in view of one's primary vocation, by which they mainly meant a father's obligation to earn money to support a family. When we open up primary vocation to include work that is disproportionately done by women in the home, we find there are many obligations that complicate the taking of a pure vegetarian stance. While very few people "need" to eat meat, families and community are fundamental human goods. Our realization of basic human goods is always partial because they so often conflict, and inevitably we will have to choose: For whom will we have the most compassion today? Sometimes it will be animals but other times it may the teenager who would enjoy some time with the family if it included chicken pot pie, and though at times it may be possible to sneak in a soy substitute or buy free range bird, at other times, it just may not be.

Tragically, sometimes efforts to lessen cooperation with this evil force us to lose opportunities to do good. Though these goods may not seem to be "grave reasons" in the context of Catholic moral theology, by viewing eating as a social practice, it becomes clear that feeding

---

[88] James T. Bretzke, *A Morally Complex World: Engaging Contemporary Moral Theology* (Collegeville: Liturgical, 2004), 118-20.

[89] Stephen H. Webb, *Good Eating* (Grand Rapids, MI: Brazos, 2001), 81, 226-28.

people and partaking in their hospitality are fundamental to human community. While those who have adopted vegetarianism or an absolute stand against eating factory-farmed meat legitimately hope for another world, the Catholic moral tradition at its best makes room for this complexity and allows for limited cooperation with evil while constantly calling for greater cooperation with good. A flexitarian stance is an ethical option that allows people to balance conflicting goods as they begin to imagine a different world.

Journal of Moral Theology, Vol. 3, No. 2 (2014): 54-71

The Use of Non-Human Animals in Biomedical Research: Can Moral Theology Fill the Gap?

Charles C. Camosy and Susan Kopp

NON-HUMAN ANIMALS constitute a massive proportion of biomedical research (BMR) subjects, with estimates of more than 25 million used in US laboratories each year.[1] From drug safety studies on rats, pet food trials on dogs, and chemotherapy testing on pigs, to the creation of inbred and genetically modified lines of mice, BMR has relied on the use of animals for many decades. Serious concern about laboratory animal use and the need for greater regulation came increasingly to the forefront beginning in the 1960s—not least because of several high profile exposés surrounding animal research and procurement of animals,[2] as well as the changing place of companion animals in our homes and in the broader culture.

Perhaps the foundational document for the developing animal rights movement was Peter Singer's 1975 international best-seller, *Animal Liberation*.[3] In part because this text was written by a secularist like Singer, and also because of the secularization of bioethics more generally, the categories used to evaluate morally the use of animals in BMR have been those of secular, post-Enlightenment modernity. Such categories avoid thick theological and metaphysical ideas in an attempt to win the assent of a (relatively) plural public sphere. It is a discourse most at home when discussing pain, pleasure, interests, preferences, autonomy, rationality, freedom, self-awareness, and cost-benefit analysis.

---

[1] The Hastings Center, "Fact Sheet: Animals Used in Research in the U.S.," www.animalresearch.thehastingscenter.org/facts-sheets/animals-used-in-research-in-the-united-states/.

[2] Bernard E. Rollin, "The Regulation of Animal Research and the Emergence of Animal Ethics: A Conceptual History," *Theoretical Medicine and Bioethics* 27, no. 4 (2006): 286-304.

[3] Peter Singer, *Animal Liberation*, (New York: Avon Books, 1975). It should be mentioned that Singer himself would likely reject any metaphysical (as opposed to legal) notion of animal rights. While his utilitarianism represents one important strand of the secular categories we have in mind, we will also engage more autonomy and rights based approaches.

A fair-minded person must admit that this discourse, together with regulatory legislation and sincere efforts on the part of animal care professionals, has produced much good. It must also be admitted, however, that some new and changing trends in animal use lie along a substantially different trajectory. Biomedical techniques (such as insertion of mobile telemetry units for data collection into genetically altered mice[4]), perhaps unimaginable even two decades ago, are now becoming commonplace in contemporary research labs.[5]

Important for our purposes in this article, these emerging areas of animal use in BMR seem to avoid the moral critiques of secular moral categories and ideas mentioned above. However, the general public still has negative moral reactions to these new practices, such as the deliberate creation of animal strains with certain diseases built into their genetic code, human/animal chimeras, and even animals with an altered sense perception in order to spare these same animals the pain and suffering that research or animal production itself might otherwise provoke.[6]

We argue that the urgent moral questions raised by these recent developments in BMR may require the theological and metaphysical concepts that our secular discourse tries to avoid. There is an important opportunity, therefore, for moral theology to fill the gap between the public's views of these matters and the moral ideas and language they have available to express these views. We propose that an adequately considered understanding of the kinds of beings that animals are, and our moral obligation to allow them to flourish precisely as these beings, underlie many negative intuitions about new and emerging uses

---

[4] Small telemetry units can be surgically implanted, for example, in the abdomens of mice and rats, with attached sensors inserted in the animal's aorta that relay information on physiological values such as heart rate or blood glucose levels to a remote receiver attached to a computer. Thus, data can be collected from animals on a continuous, real-time basis. The PhysioTel™ Hybrid Digital (HD) implant manufactured by Data Sciences International (DSI), is one such example of these units, with videos of these telemetry units currently available on the company's website and Youtube. See www.datasci.com/glucose/product-information/implant-able-telemetry-overview.

[5] Increases in numbers of small rodents can be seen corresponding to the development and use of new strains of genetically altered mice. For example, between the period 2001 and 2012, the 2012 Home Office of the UK document, *Annual Statistics of Scientific Procedures on Living Animals* , cites more than a 35% annual jump in use of these mice (increase of approximately 1 million annually). Home Office of the Government of the United Kingdom, "Annual Statistics of Scientific Procedures on Living Animals (2012)," www.gov.uk/government/-publications/statistics-of-scientific-procedures-on-living-animals-great-britain-2012.

[6] For more in-depth discussion of this issue, see C.A. Schuppli and D.M. Weary, "Attitudes towards the use of genetically modified animals in research," *Public Understanding of Science 19* (November 2010): 686-697, and Paul B. Thompson, "The Opposite of Human Enhancement: Nanotechnology and the Blind Chicken Problem," *Nanoethics* 2 (2008):305-316.

and techniques on animals in BMR—and can even help create a framework for ongoing moral analysis of these practices. We also claim that, without careful attention to the idolatries of consumerism and extending human life, our culture will continue to fail to provide adequate protection of non-human animals in such research settings.

Use of Animals in BMR: Regulatory Achievements

We will see below that some of the most important and recent secular regulatory achievements—particularly with regard to primates—rely on concepts like freedom, autonomy, and self-determination. Others appeal to a utilitarian analysis: how much pain and distress[7] does a particular research project inflict on the animals being used?[8] Does it affect the interests or preferences they may have? Do the benefits for human beings outweigh the costs to these animals?

Utilitarian categories and analyses may be problematic for moral theologians, but one could hardly deny the good things this approach has achieved. Indeed, it was this kind of analysis—and (sadly) not moral theology—that brought the question of moral concern for animals to the fore in Western culture. It has convinced our culture that the moral claims animals make on humans are such that, at a minimum, we should spend significant resources to make research more humane. In some contexts, such as those which require the use of primates, much of the Western world believes that we ought not to use animals at all.[9]

Current guidelines for regulation and care of laboratory animals in the United States have their foundation in the federal Animal Welfare

---

[7] An in-depth discussion of the very complex questions around pain and distress in animals is beyond the scope of this article. However, growing understandings of animal anatomy and physiology are indicating that many different species of animals must "feel" or perceive pain in some sense. Much has been learned, in particular, about the surprising similarities in the way neurological systems function in mammals. A shift is taking place that considers not only the sensory aspect of physical pain but also the possibility of "emotional or conscious" components to an animal's pain linked to memory and the capacity for more complex thought patterns (even if some philosophers of biology have been more cautious, noting that we just have no access to the conscious experiences of other animals).

[8] Terms such as "distress," "consciousness," and even "suffering" are used with increasing frequency across various disciplines within veterinary medicine and animal welfare science, and are reflective of a trend both in veterinary care and in the public's ethical concern for human and nonhuman animals. For further discussion of related terminology see the National Research Council (US), Committee on Recognition and Alleviation of Distress in Laboratory Animals, "Recognition and Alleviation of Distress in Laboratory Animals," (Washington, DC: National Acad-emies Press, 2008), 13-17, www.ncbi.nlm.nih.gov/books/NBK4032/pdf/ TOC.pdf, and Helen S. Proctor, Gemma Carder, and Amelia R. Cornish, "Searching for Animal Sentience: A Systematic Review of the Scientific Literature," *Animals* 2 (2013): 882-906, www.mdpi.com/2076-2615/3/3/882.

[9] Only Gabon and the US still actively use chimpanzees in research.

Act (AWA) approved by Congress in 1966. It became a more formidable obstacle to improper research practices on animals in the 1980s with several key amendments, including oversight powers given directly to the United States Department of Agriculture, Animal and Plant Health Inspection Service. Additionally, all government-funded research under the Health and Human Services' Public Health Services Grants (PHS) became subject to further regulation through more restrictive guidelines covering mice, rats, and birds—in addition to higher functioning mammals. The focus of such regulations was consistently on protecting animals from undue suffering—and although mice, rats, and birds are not regulated under the AWA, protection of these species is mandated for all institutions receiving federal funding through PHS, and most notably for all projects funded by the National Institutes of Health (NIH).[10]

Under the AWA and federally mandated PHS guidelines, institutions doing research on animals are required to create and employ Institutional Animal Care and Use Committees (IACUC).[11] These interdisciplinary panels include an attending veterinarian of the institution, scientists, and at least one outside member not affiliated with the institution. IACUCs have a mandate to ensure regulatory compliance around animal housing and care and to ensure that all persons working with animals are properly trained, as well as an obligation to respond to any complaints concerning care of animals in the facility. But, perhaps most important, the IACUC approves, and periodically renews approval, of all research projects using animals covered and protected under these various regulations, with power to suspend or terminate projects that fail to meet prior IACUC approved research protocol standards.

In the early stage of a research project's development, even before researchers secure funding, formal protocol proposals must first be submitted to the respective institution's IACUC for approval. Regulations have become progressively more extensive, such as requiring documentation of a new project's likelihood to evoke pain or distress, detailed descriptions of planned housing, and assurance of enriched

---

[10] Specific information regarding IACUCs and requirements for researchers and research protocols mentioned here can be found in the United State Department of Agriculture, "Animal Welfare Act and Animal Welfare Regulations"(2013), www.aphis.usda.gov/animal_welfare/downloads/Animal%20Care%20Blue%20Book%20-%202013%20-%20FINAL.pdf, and the National Research Council (US) Committee for the Update of the Guide for the Care and Use of Laboratory Animals, "Guide for the Care and Use of Laboratory Animals," National Academies Press (2011), www.ncbi.nlm.nih.gov/books/NBK54050/.

[11] United State Department of Agriculture, "Animal Welfare Act and Animal Welfare Regulations," (2013): 32, www.aphis.usda.gov/animal_welfare/downloads/Animal%20Care%20Blue%20Book%20-%202013%20-%20FINAL.pdf.

environments for the animal subjects. Use of pain medications, for example, is standard practice and protocols can be suspended if such administration is not adhered to. Researchers are also required to document any prior, similar studies relating to their own proposed project, in the hopes of eliminating redundant use of animals. Similarly, a rationale for the number of animals to be used, along with a detailed literature search for possible alternatives to the use of animals, must also be submitted. A researcher must justify, for example, why he or she intends to use dogs in a new drug trial—rather than invertebrate species or live tissue cultures grown in the laboratory—before a project will be approved.[12]

An important limitation, however, presents itself when attempts are made to determine harm/risk vs. benefits of the research. While goals of a given project must be clearly stated, together with what are termed "humane endpoints" (pre-established criteria during the course of research whereby animal pain or distress must be relieved or the experiment terminated due to decreased welfare and well-being),[13] attempts to assess and balance risks and benefits can be difficult. Some believe there is need for more effective frameworks around questions regarding the balance between harm to animals and benefit to medical and scientific progress.[14]

The overall focus on animal welfare in animal experimental design is increasingly summarized by referencing the "3 R's"—*Reduction* (minimum number of animals needed for viable results), *Refinement* (modifying new and existing experimental protocols to ensure minimal pain and distress to animals used and improve quality of life), and *Replacement* (with non-living animal tissue models, or animal species considered lower on the evolutionary scale).[15] A significant number of universities and institutions now employ 3R experts to ensure sufficient priority is given to related animal welfare concerns.[16] Some have been frustrated with the pace with which 3R strategies have been employed, but there has been slow but significant progress in recent decades with respect to care and treatment of animals used in research.[17]

---

[12] See later mention in this article of the 3 R's and the mandate for "Replacement" of animals higher on the evolutionary scale whenever possible.

[13] National Research Council, "Guide for the Care and Use of Laboratory Animals," National Academies Press," 27.

[14] For a good overview, see: Stephen R. Latham, "U.S. Law and Animal Experimentation: A Critical Primer," *Hastings Center Report 42: Sp. Issue (2012):* 35-9.

[15] For more on the 3 R's, see USDA National Agricultural Library 3 R's website: http://awic.nal.usda.gov/alternatives/3rs.

[16] Susan Kopp, "Training the Next Generation," *Hastings Center Report 42: Sp. Issue (2012):* 19-22.

[17] Viktor Reinhardt, ed., *Caring Hands: Discussions by the Laboratory Animal Refinement and Enrichment Forum,* vol. II (Washington, DC: Animal Welfare Institute, 2010). This book is a striking collection of ideas, recommendations, anecdotes,

Susan Kopp, in working closely with research animal care professionals for more than a decade, has consistently noted the deep level of care and concern shown by these colleagues in their dealings with laboratory animals on a daily basis. Hard-won animal welfare changes have come not only as a result of animal protection groups but also through the efforts of those working in the laboratory animal care field itself. Indeed, the culture of care for animals in research settings today is often one which surpasses the minimum required standards set by the government.[18]

Regulation of the Use of Primates in BMR

Beyond a utilitarian focus on pleasure and pain and cost/harm vs. benefit, the secular Enlightenment has also focused on the concepts of the autonomy, freedom, rationality, and self-determination of individuals. Though at first used to explain the dignity and rights of human beings, the work of Peter Singer, Jane Goodall, and others has drawn very public attention to the fact that certain animals—and especially primates—also have something like these traits. Their ability to recognize themselves in a mirror, for instance, demonstrates self-awareness. Primates also have complex social capabilities like causal inference and deception. They are capable of understanding, using, and even teaching (to their children) hundreds of words in American Sign Language. Through this language, several primates have revealed their rich emotional lives—including friendship acquisition and loss, excited anticipation of birthdays and Christmas, and even frustration and anger in response to unfair treatment.[19]

As these capabilities became more widely known, public pressure to reconsider use of chimpanzees grew. In 2010, the NIH commissioned a study by the Institute of Medicine (IOM) to assess ongoing needs for chimpanzee use in biomedical and behavioral research. The IOM's final report, *Chimpanzees in Biomedical and Behavioral Research: Assessing the Necessity*,[20] urged major restrictions on use of chimpanzees, which were accepted by NIH and are resulting in the retirement from research of a vast majority of such government-owned animals.

---

and discussions by laboratory animal care professionals centered on their many efforts to improve and enrich the lives of laboratory animals entrusted to their care.

[18] H.J. Klein and K.A. Bayne, "Establishing a culture of care, conscience, and responsibility: addressing the improvement of scientific discovery and animal welfare through science-based performance standards," *ILAR Journal* 48, no. 1 (2007): 3-11.

[19] The fact that primates have these capabilities is generally well-known, but a nice clearinghouse for articles, videos, testimonies and other references for their being present in gorillas has been created at koko.org.

[20] Institute of Medicine (IOM) of the National Academies, "Chimpanzees in Biomedical and Behavioral Research: Assessing the Necessity," (2011), www.nap.edu/catalog.php?record_id=13257.

The IOM report claims that use of chimpanzees, because of their close genetic proximity to humans (as well as their biological and behavioral traits), requires that we provide a much higher standard of justification for their use in research.[21] The report also acknowledges that their recommendation was further based on the availability of new and viable biotechnological alternatives to chimpanzee use, such as cell-based technologies and other non-primate animal models.[22] To use chimpanzees, researchers must be able to show not only a strong need for such testing at the level of public health concern with no other viable alternative to chimpanzee use, but they must also show that it cannot be ethically carried out on human beings. On this last point, Jeffrey Kahn notes, in *The Hastings Center Report*: "[T]hat human subjects must be ruled out on ethical grounds as part of the justification for the use of chimpanzees turns the traditional presumption regarding the use of research animals on its head."[23]

But, in some ways, restricting use of primates was a relatively easy call. Broad public support was already there, and central secular moral categories of self-determination, autonomy, and self-awareness have already been applied to these creatures. However, the same cannot be said of other less sophisticated species, for which use is increasing dramatically in BMR sectors.[24] As we will see below, moral evaluation of the use of these animals requires a framework substantially different from the one which led to restriction of research on primates.

Advances in Biotechnological Research on Smaller Animals

Increasing use of smaller animals in BMR has coincided with game-changing advances in biotechnology. It has become commonplace in recent years, for instance, to manipulate cellular DNA of mice to create new genetic lines which will develop early onset diabetes, neuromuscular disease, or obesity. This can involve both inbreeding and direct manipulation of genes, including insertion of new gene sequences from the same or other species, or the functional removal of other genes.[25] Paul Root Wolpe characterizes this altering of ge-

---

[21] Institute of Medicine, "Chimpanzees," 28-29.

[22] Institute of Medicine, "Chimpanzees," 66.

[23] Jeffrey Kahn, "Raising the Bar: The Implications of the IOM Report on the Use of Chimpanzees in Research," *Hastings Center Report 42: Sp. Issue (2012):* 27-30.

[24] Home Office of the UK, "Annual Statistics."

[25] Mice, for example, who receive pieces of DNA from other animal species, including human DNA, are called "transgenic mice." Instead, gene targeting that eliminates the functional role of other genes on a chromosome using genetic engineering techniques creates new lines of so-called "knockout mice." Both are considered genetically engineered animals and this type of technology, together with repetitive inbreeding techniques, is responsible for the large and varied numbers of mouse lines currently available for purchase and use.

nomes as a "third wave" of planetary evolution—beyond natural selection and the selective breeding practices used by humankind for centuries.[26]

It is of particular interest that the development and use of genetically modified animals (and mice in particular) often requires huge numbers of animals, many of whom are generated as a "collateral" part of a process aimed at generating new, homogeneous strains of mice for needed studies. The UK, for instance, saw a 9% increase in the number of animals used for biomedical research during 2012, including a 14% increase in mice, mostly for transgenic research.[27] Tellingly, the number of procedures on genetically modified animals now outnumbers "ordinary" research animal use for the first time in history.[28]

Shifts toward this kind of research have been rapid, not only because of the significant potential for medical and scientific progress, but also because of the quest for profit. Biotechnology, and specifically biotechnological use of animals, now plays a key role in the portfolios of both private and public investors.[29] While there is a sincere effort on the part of many in animal research to move toward the 3 R's, the potential profit from these new biotechnological techniques is pulling demand for laboratory animals (and especially mice and rats) in a very different direction, with broad-reaching negative impacts for animals.

Consider the plight of genetically engineered animals. Researchers today not only can order mice who have been genetically created to develop diabetes at a young age, but also have the option to order pre-prepared "obese" specimens obtained through deliberate overfeeding before shipment.[30] Repeated inbreeding of other lines of mice has also, for example, created hairless animals lacking a thymus gland—for use in studies where researchers desire mice with decreased immunity. So varied are the commercial lines of engineered mice, numbering in the

---

[26] Paul Root Wolpe, "It's time to question bio-engineering," TED Talk (Nov. 2010), www.ted.com/talks/paul_root_wolpe_it_s_time_to_question_bio_engineering.html.

[27] Home Office of the UK, "Annual Statistics."

[28] Home Office of the UK, "Annual Statistics." See also www.understandinganimalresearch.org.uk/news/2013/07/2012-animal-research-statistics-from-the-home-office/.

[29] One example is Texas based Lexicon Pharmaceuticals (www.lexgen.com), founded in 1995, for human drug development using knockout mice engineering techniques. The company also collaborates with other major pharmaceutical and biotech companies such as Genentech and Bristol-Myers Squibb.

[30] A number of biotech companies offer laboratory animals by design, with additional specialized services and feeding regiments. As an example, see The Jackson Laboratory Diet-Induced Obesity (mouse) Models: www.jaxmice.jax.org/diomice/dioguide.html.

thousands,[31] that one major institution has a website for researchers to request the production of specific transgenic, knockout, or other strains according to their project needs. The photo of four tiny mouse pups on the web page has the caption "Make My Mouse!"[32] One cannot help but note that, in this context, animals seemingly have become a pure commodity—able to be assembled, redesigned, modified, bought, and sold.

Biotechnological capabilities also impact researchers by increasingly providing them with added options for purchasing surgical interventions on animals prior to arrival in their laboratories. In this regard, it is now possible to purchase rats with adrenal glands or pancreas already removed for endocrinology studies. Guinea pigs can be ordered with blood pressure monitoring devices implanted in their aortas and cannulas in their brains. Reusable telemetry units can even be pre-deposited in the abdomens of young mice and rats to make it easier to collect data on vital signs and other physical parameters.

Consider also that a rat model for dementia is now available for purchase and delivery. The "Samaritan Alzheimer's Rat Model™"—rather than genetically manipulating animals (which is also available) to induce Alzheimer's—is created by surgically implanting a slow release pump system that injects the rat's left brain ventricle with an iron containing peptide, causing sufficient brain changes that mimic Alzheimer's symptoms. According to the company website, visible signs of dementia can be seen as rapidly as four weeks after initial administration of the chemical.[33]

Many understandably have a viscerally negative response to these kinds of interventions, but a serious attempt to call them into question requires going beyond this. Our secular discourse, when attempting to defend the moral value of mice and rats, cannot invoke the sophisticated traits used to highlight the value of primates. Instead, there has been an almost exclusive focus on utilitarian concerns for pain and suffering—with some related attention paid to providing species-specific social housing, environmental enrichment, etc. Whether it is the kind of negative life issues involved with early development of diabetes or dementia, or the placement of abdominal monitors in mice prior to shipment, a secular utilitarian approach insists that burdens on the animals must be played off against projected benefits.

---

[31] T. J. Fielder, L. Barrios et al., "A survey to establish performance standards for the production of transgenic mice," *Transgenic Research* 19, no. 4 (August 2010): 675-81.

[32] "Make My Mouse!," UC Davis Mouse Biology Program, www.mousebiology.org/help/makemice.php.

[33] Taconic Farms, Inc., "Samaritan Alzheimer's Rat Model™ FAB Datasheet," www.taconic.com/user-assets/documents/samaritanfabdatasheet.pdf.

BEYOND PAIN AND SUFFERING

We argue that offering sufficient justification for questioning recent trends in the biotechnological use of animals must go beyond a secular utilitarian ethical framework. For instance, some argue that we just don't have the kind of access to the experiential lives of mice and rats necessary for determining if they actually suffer.[34] Furthermore, one could reasonably argue on utilitarian grounds that, whatever pain or suffering research animals may feel in these settings, it is far outweighed by the value of reducing the more important pain and suffering felt by humans. This argument is even more applicable to creatures that don't have a mammalian nervous system, such as the increasingly used zebra fish.

Or suppose we create new kinds of genetically-modified mice and rats who are incapable of feeling pain. Perhaps we can modify development of brain regions that process information from nerve endings, or figure out how to deaden the nerve endings themselves. Or perhaps we could alter mouse and rat brains in such a way as to keep them alive in a semi- or unconscious state so that when we surgically remove organs before sale to a research lab—or during the course of their development of neuromuscular disease—we could claim they do not suffer. We could alter the animal's ability to access memories related to fear and anxiety, or even trigger a neural tube defect such that laboratory-bred mice and rats were born with only a brain stem and no higher brain function at all.[35]

---

[34] Shifts are being seen in scientific literature, as noted prior, in speaking of an animal's overall "well-being" or quality of life. Physical pain from a fracture, for example, causes stimulation of pain pathways leading to what is thought to be something like pain perception. But, in addition, the animal may experience anxiety and fear on top of that pain, such as during repeated handling by veterinary personnel for treatment. All can be seen as stressors that negatively impact the animal, resulting in additive distress and suffering in addition to physical pain itself.

Stress, generally considered an organism's physical or psychological response to stimuli around it requiring it to alter its activity or actions, or overall behavior, may be negative or positive. When negative stressors alter an organism's behavior to the point that it can no longer adapt, affecting its potential for survival, the organism is said to be in a state of distress. Distress can be short-term or of prolonged duration and can sometimes have multiple meanings. Some animal ethicists include the inability of an animal to perform natural, species specific behaviors as a stressor that impacts an animal negatively, thus causing it to be in a state of long-term distress, even if signs of that distress may not always be easily visible.

[35] There has also been significant secular discourse around *telos* and the intentional engineering of animals such that they will not feel pain or, alternatively, might continue to be bred for traits such as blindness (in the case of chickens) in order to remain undisturbed by overcrowding and related housing concerns. For more detailed discussions of these issues, see Bernard E. Rollin's "Télos, conservation of welfare, and ethical issues in genetic engineering of animals" *Current Topics in Neurosciences* (2014): 1-18, and Paul B. Thompson, "Opposite of Human Enhancement."

Furthermore, many advances in biotechnology may neither cause nor alleviate pain and nevertheless raise serious ethical questions. It is not clear, for instance, to what degree genetically-altered mice and rats, engineered to be born without a pancreas or adrenal glands, will experience pain or suffering along the course of their lives. Nor is it clear that human/non-human chimeras—such as neonatal animals serving as a kind of growth media for development of new human pancreas and kidneys for transplantation—experience pain or discomfort.[36] Furthermore, with the development of new pain medications and refinements of current research protocols, biotechnological advances also allow that some genetic manipulations and experimentation can be conducted without significant pain or suffering.

It is also important to note that even when this research avoids some of the concerns of our secular discourse, the general public has serious moral concerns about biotechnological modifications and use of animals in scientific research.[37] As ethicist Bernard Rollin points out, our culture wants to be sure that basic needs and the "nature" of each animal are respected. Rollin believes that there is a societal expectation that use of animals will "embody respect and provision for their psychological needs and natures."[38]

We have a significant gap, therefore, between (1) moral skepticism about these practices on the part of the general public and (2) the moral ideas and language the public has available to adequately and effectively articulate this skepticism.

Bridging the Gap: Enter Moral Theology

Although an inclusive public sphere is a good thing, the downside of thinning out our secular moral discourse has been well-documented by theologians and others.[39] In attempting to appeal to the least common denominator in our plural culture—and ridding it of any (explicitly) theological content—we have impoverished our capacity to respond to many of today's most pressing moral concerns. Recent developments in biotechnology in general, and the use of animals in particular, are classic instances in which our secular culture finds itself

---

[36] Hitomi Matsunari, Hiroshi Nagashima, et al., "Blastocyst complementation generates exogenic pancreas in vivo in apancreatic cloned pigs," *Proceedings of the National Academy of Sciences USA* (March 19, 2013), www.ncbi.nlm.nih.gov/pmc/ articles/PMC3607052/.

[37] C.A. Schuppli and D.M. Weary, "Attitudes towards the use of genetically modified animals in research."

[38] Bernard E. Rollin, "Animal Rights as a Mainstream Phenomenon," *Animals* 1, no. 1 (2011): 102-15.

[39] The number of thinkers who have pointed this out are too numerous to name, but two classic works are by Alasdair MacIntyre, *After Virtue* (Notre Dame: University of Notre Dame Press, 1981) and Stanley Hauerwas, *Resident Aliens* (Nashville: Abington Press, 1989).

without the necessarily thick moral claims to articulate our ethical concerns. But moral theology, which reflects a rich tradition spanning many centuries, has the kind of understanding of the good required to articulate them.

For our purposes in this article, the most important aspect of moral theology to highlight is the metaphysical concept of teleology. For Christians, the very first pages of the Bible explain that non-human animals were created "good" by God independent of any instrumental value they may have for us. An animal is different from a hammer, for instance, because a hammer has been created for one purpose: to be a tool for human beings. It has no intrinsic goodness apart from this instrumental value. By contrast, God created animals "good," *period*, to flourish in their own right as the good kinds of things that they are. We cannot instrumentalize them the way we do hammers. Each animal has her own nature or *telos* which God intends each creature to achieve in his or her fullness. Indeed, Sacred Scripture explains that salvation will result in a new heaven and a new earth in which *all* creatures (not just humans) will be redeemed and live out their most flourishing selves.[40]

David Clough, explaining how secular utilitarians find themselves unable articulate the concept of an animal's teleology, puts it this way:

> Last week I found a young bird dead at our doorstep. My response was one of sadness, not because the bird at the moment of its death had a preference for its life to continue, nor because its parents would currently be grieving its loss, neither of which may be true, but because I had a sense of the life ahead of this poor creature, of its growth to maturity and the particular contribution it should have made to the universe of creaturely life.... The death of that young bird is sad not because preferences went unmet, or the sum of happiness was infinitesimally diminished, but because this one life did not reach the end to which it was ordered.[41]

Some Christians mistakenly believe that the dominion over creation that God gave to human beings means that we may treat animals as

---

[40] In the modern day animal and veterinary ethics arena, ethicist Bernard E. Rollin is at the forefront in speaking about animal *telos,* while also giving priority to animal avoidance of pain and suffering. Rollin does not rule out genetic engineering and modification of research animals that might alter the animals' *telos,* if the end result would yield a further minimization of such pain and suffering, and the animal were to be no worse off as a result. See "Telos, conservation of welfare, and ethical issues in genetic engineering of animals."

[41] David Clough, "How to Respect Other Animals: Lesson for Theology from Peter Singer and *Vice Versa*" in *God, the Good and Utilitarianism*, ed. John Perry (Oxford: Oxford University Press, 2014), 173.

mere tools, ignoring the kind of flourishing God intended for each one. On the contrary, Pope John Paul II insists that "dominion granted to man by the Creator is not an absolute power, nor can one speak of a freedom to 'use and misuse', or to dispose of things as one pleases."[42] To no one's surprise, *The Catechism of the Catholic Church*[43] reflects John Paul's view, insisting that:

> Creatures exist only in dependence on each other, to complete each other, in the service of each other…. (no. 338)
> There is a solidarity among all creatures arising from the fact that all have the same Creator and are all ordered to his glory. (no. 344)

In a July 2001 message to a Pontifical Academy for Life meeting on xenotransplantation (animal transplantation in humans), the Pope spoke of the new scientific and ethical problems before us. While affirming in his message the possibility of using animals for organ donation in humans, he also spoke of the necessity for "attentive consideration for animals."[44]

Pope Benedict XVI may have taken the implications of animal teleology even more seriously than did his predecessor. In his encyclical *Caritas in Veritate*, for instance, Benedict insists that we must avoid aiming

> at total technical dominion over nature, because the natural environment is more than raw material to be manipulated at our pleasure; it is a wondrous work of the Creator containing a "grammar" which sets forth ends and criteria for its wise use, not its reckless exploitation.[45]

Pope Francis seems to be on a similar path, not least because, as this article went to press, we received confirmation of his upcoming encyclical focused on ecological concern. Several lines in his Apostolic Exhortation *Evangelli Gaudium* may preview his more developed thoughts to come:

> There are other weak and defenseless beings who are frequently at the mercy of economic interests or indiscriminate exploitation. I am speaking of creation as a whole. We human beings are not only the beneficiaries but also the stewards of other creatures.[46]

---

[42] John Paul II, *Sollicitudo Rei Socialis* (1988), nos. 1-2, 34.
[43] *Catechism of the Catholic Church*, 2nd Ed. (Libreria Editrice Vaticana, 2000).
[44] John Paul II, "Message to A Congress Organized by the Pontifical Academy for Life on the Justness of Xenotransplantation," (July 1, 2001), http://www.vatican.va/-holy_father/john_paul_ii/speeches/2001/documents/hf_jp-ii_spe_20010702_pc-life_en.html.
[45] Benedict XVI, *Caritas in Veritate* (2009), no. 48.
[46] Francis. *Evangelii Gaudium* (2014), no. 215.

Theological Insights about Animal Teleology

The Church's view of animal teleology, coming directly from a thick, explicitly metaphysical understanding of the good, is in turn grounded in a theological narrative or story about creation and its relationship to its Creator. But can the insights of this approach be heard in contemporary secular discussions on the use of animals in BMR? Catholic moral theology, especially insofar as it has built on the insights of Aristotle and St. Thomas Aquinas, has been widely-concerned with teleology for many centuries. But one of the most important moral theologians to focus on this topic in recent years did so in light of some shifting views in biology and the philosophy of biology. In her important book, *Nature as Reason,* Jean Porter is quite aware that many in the sciences are skeptical about the metaphysical idea that a mouse or rat has a nature or *telos*.[47] After all, don't the most recent insights about evolution resist ideas like "the" good or flourishing of an animal? In response to this concern, Porter notes that this standard view has been challenged by a number of biologists and philosophers of science, who "have begun to argue for the legitimacy and indeed the necessity of incorporating certain kinds of teleological analysis into the biological sciences."[48]

It seems perfectly obvious, for instance, that "natural kinds of living creatures" do in fact "seem to exist in nature."[49] The existence of such natural kinds

> implies that recognizable kinds of creatures exhibit intelligible similarities, and relate to one another in orderly ways.... [T]he diverse kinds of living creatures are not just a set of random groupings—they constitute an *ordered* set of natural kinds. And it is difficult to see how this ordering can be entirely the result of random chance.

But isn't evolution a random process? Porter denies that one can conclude something about evolution's randomness merely from random interactions of genetic material, or even from such interactions at a molecular or atomic level. Many contemporary biologists—including Richard Lewontin, author of *The Triple Helix*[50]—point out that "the genes by themselves do not even determine their expression in an individual creature" and cannot account for all the processes through which kinds of creatures develop and evolve.[51]

---

[47] Jean Porter, *Nature as Reason: A Thomistic Theory of the Natural Law* (Grand Rapids: Eerdmans, 2005). For a similar take, see also Celia Deane-Drummond's *Ethics of Nature* (Malden, MA: Wiley-Blackwell, 2004).
[48] Porter, *Nature as Reason*, 420.
[49] Porter, *Nature as Reason*, 90.
[50] Richard C. Lewontin, *The Triple Helix: Gene, Organism, and Environment* (Cambridge, MA.: Harvard University Press, 2000), 136.
[51] Porter, *Nature as Reason*, 94.

Important for our purposes in this article, Porter insists that a teleological understanding of animals does not require theism:

> Teleological language does not imply any reference to externally imposed purposes, whether ours, those of some demiurge or creator, or a generalized nature or evolutionary process. Rather, in this context the language of purpose functions in such a way as to render the different components of a living creature intelligible, in terms of the contributions to the life processes of the creature…. [T]he observation that the eye is meant for seeing does not presuppose a story about the way the physical mechanism of the eye reflects the contrivance of an omnipotent designer…. Rather, it presupposes a more straightforward account of the role the eye plays in promoting the overall well-being of the creature.[52]

Porter claims that most of us know animals have a *telos* simply at the level of intuition. This is what allows us to discern what it means to be a healthy and flourishing creature, as opposed to one who is sick and declining. These judgments, says Porter, are "fundamental to functioning in the world," and she claims it is "absurd" to argue they are "wholly the product of cultural construction."[53]

And it isn't just abstract theorists like philosophers of biology or moral theologians who take the view that the animal kingdom is made up of natural kinds, each with a nature and *telos* that we are bound to respect. More and more animal welfare specialists insist that, if we are to use animals, their "species-specific" needs and behaviors must be met.[54] Such considerations range from the simple provision of nesting materials and nest boxes for pregnant rats to assurance that a species of monkey, because of its typical social structure in the wild, should never be housed in an isolated fashion. It is difficult to miss the similarity these considerations have with respect to the flourishing of these animals as the kinds of beings they are.

Implications for Biotechnological Use of Animals

The ethic we advance in this article insists that animals are "good" independent of the concerns of human beings. The way they express this goodness is by flourishing as the kinds of beings they are—by living out their nature or *telos*. Though much has been achieved with secular frameworks which invoke interests, self-determination, rationality, self-awareness, and pain/suffering, we argue that it is necessary to consider the flourishing of the whole creature as the kind of thing it

[52] Porter, *Nature as Reason*, 100.

[53] Porter, *Nature as Reason*, 101-2.

[54] Numerous references, for example, to species-specific parameters can be found in the National Research Council's important "Guide for the Care and Use of Laboratory Animals."

is. Doing so has significant ethical implications for recent developments in the biotechnological use of animals—and in particular for increasingly invasive surgical procedures and alterations of genomes that affect an animal's ability to flourish. Every use and alteration of an animal in this context must respect the moral claim that the nature of that animal makes upon our behavior and on our moral duty to allow it to flourish as the kind of thing that it is, without reducing him or her to a mere tool or commodity.

This kind of framework provides a moral vocabulary for our broader culture to use when articulating its skepticism about the current trajectory of animal use in BMR. Though a particular intervention may not cause pain or suffering (and may even be designed to alleviate it), if the research protect refuses to allow an animal to flourish as the kind of being it is, then it should be subject to moral critique.

Conclusions and Questions for Further Study

The fundamental theological distinction is between Creator and creation. Christians believe that the dominion God has given us over creation has limits and obligations, including the duty to respect the lives of non-human animals as "good" independent of human concerns or priorities. We misunderstand this fundamental truth when corporate profit—or even preservation of our own lives—idolatrously trumps God's will that each animal flourish as the kind of being that it is.

This insight has significant implications for researchers, research institutions, and consumers—especially if they identify as Christian. As we have seen above, recent and emerging biotechnological research has given us the ability to do once unimaginable things to animals. Seemingly with each news cycle, we brush up against new thresholds and the pace of our ethical reflection struggles to keep up. Charles Camosy recently attended a conference in which one cutting-edge biotech researcher mentioned in his remarks that "there is no time to pause and reflect on what you are doing—only time to think about the next research grant." If BMR is engaged by a significant number of researchers working within corporate and institutional structures which make it difficult for them to consider their professional ethical duties towards other living creatures, then we argue that these structures must be critically examined and reformed.

The present moment in biotechnological research provides an important opportunity for both religious and secular communities to bring their unique insights to the table. If authentic and lasting reform is going to happen, it must be based on the collaborative efforts of these groups at the highest levels. Conversation about the moral implications of animal teleology is particularly promising in this regard. We propose that there is much room for a truly diverse, interdisciplinary exploration of the moral implications of animal teleology, and we believe there is reasonable hope of finding common ground upon which to build and craft solutions to the new problems that use of animals in BMR are placing before us.

Displaying serious respect for animal teleology will mean that some major biotechnological research will be halted until thoughtful moral and ethical consideration can be properly engaged. Some research protocols may be changed to allow the research subjects to flourish as the kinds of creatures they are, but it is also likely that the added expense may price some out of the market. All researchers should be moving toward the 3 R's, but the difficult truth is that some research which uses animals should simply not be done. This may mean that we do not find (or will not find as rapidly) cures to diseases that would have otherwise been found. Human beings, at least if we are to recognize our finite biological nature, must avoid idolatrously fixating on "avoiding death" and "extending life" to the exclusion of all other goods and concerns.

Although we have come to some broad conclusions in this article, our central goal was to articulate a problem and outline a framework by which we might think about possible solutions. As such, it was beyond our scope to enter deeply into specifics for arriving at these solutions. However, we did want to conclude with some suggestions for further work in the light of our general reflections:

- We need a better framework for doing moral analyses comparing the harm done to animals with the projected benefit for humans. Utilitarianism has fundamental hurdles that look difficult to overcome, especially as it tries to weigh incommensurate goods/values. There is no scale, for instance, on which we can compare "the deaths of 100,000 mice" vs. "substantial increases in human eye health." Difficulties increase when we add respect for animal teleology into the mix.[55] We suggest that, because moral theology has engaged in proportionate reasoning for centuries (especially when it comes to issues like war/peace and removing of end-of-life care), there is now an interesting conversation to be had about how its insights might be applied to use of animals in BMR.

- Even if proportionate reasoning helps us do it more carefully, at a certain point cost-benefit analysis becomes inappropriate—especially in light of the *Catechism* proclaiming "solidarity" with all creatures. Is it possible to discover decisive endpoints and limits as to how far an experiment may proceed in its effects on an animal before it should be halted? The *Catechism* insists that it is immoral for humans to inflict suffering on animals unless it provides for a "need." But what constitutes a "need" for human beings? What does "need" mean in light of the 3 R's? Does it mean, for

[55] One possible way to think about this might claim that the more we diverge from the natural *telos* of the animal, the more perceived benefit must be at stake in the research intervention.

instance, that we have a duty to explore all other non-animal options, and use them even if they are more expensive?

- What about the effects (both negative and positive) that some biotechnological research might have on the flourishing of future animals? How might a reduction of genetic diversity due to inbreeding, or the knocking out of certain genes, impact other species, especially if biotechnologically-altered species are eventually (though inadvertently) introduced into ecosystems? How could such risk be assessed and evaluated?

- In our market-driven system, emerging biotechnological advances involving animals are often financed by the profits sought by biotech corporations. But those profits exist only because of the behavior of those who consume medical products produced by corporations which use animals in ways that severely compromise their ability to flourish. How should we think about our responsibilities (both as individuals and as institutions) to avoid those medical products produced through immoral treatment of animals? Catholic moral theology has a well-developed tradition on "cooperation with evil." Perhaps it could be developed to consider these questions.[56]

The changing use of nonhuman animals in BMR presents us with new and urgent ethical questions. By ensuring that priority is given to the teleological flourishing and good of all animals, including those living in laboratories, our culture can at least access the kind of moral framework necessary to respond to these complex questions and challenges. We believe that authentic collaboration between diverse groups representing religious and secular constituencies can light the way in finding moral pathways by which to travel in the pursuit of new scientific discoveries and medical therapies—while at the same time allowing non-human animals to flourish as the kind of beings they are. M

---

[56] Writing in this volume, Julie Hanlon Rubio has a helpful discussion of cooperation with evil and eating factory farmed meat. Her insights could serve as a starting point for thinking about cooperation with the problematic uses of animals in BMR.

Journal of Moral Theology, Vol. 3, No. 2 (2014): 72-92

Evolutionary Perspectives on Inter-Morality and Inter-Species Relationships Interrogated in the Light of the Rise and Fall of *Homo sapiens sapiens*

Celia Deane–Drummond

IF WE DEFINE "SPECIESIST" AS AN EXCESSIVE CONCERN for our own species, then it is clear that arguments could be made for accusing not just the Roman Catholic tradition, but Christianity in general and Western culture in particular of that characteristic. I will argue as a prolegomena to this paper that the presupposition of "speciesism" is a concern to protect human beings.[1] But in the first section I will argue that exclusive concern for humanity is not *necessary* for that protection, any more than widening our moral concern to include those outside our immediate family or nation somehow threatens familial commitments or national loyalties. Indeed ignoring wider issues fails to take into account interwoven relationships at different social levels. The utilitarian moral presuppositions embedded in particular accounts of animal rights from which the accusation of Christianity as speciesist first arose need to be distinguished from whether other animals are worthy of moral consideration.

In the second section, I discuss how "speciesist" viewpoints are often associated with fear of evolutionary explanations of human nature. Since evolutionary accounts inevitably weaken the idea of radically distinct kinds, and thus blur the boundary between humans and other creatures, they seem to undercut human distinctiveness. Since the more strident evolutionary accounts push evolution as an explanatory tool for all aspects of human becoming (including morality and religion), it is no surprise that such views seem threatening to standard Catholic moral theology, with its emphasis on human dignity in general and the uniqueness of the human person in particular. I will offer a critique of the evolutionary accounts of human morality that presuppose strong evolutionary naturalism.

In the third section, I defend a suitably qualified evolutionary account, one that take proper account of the significance of the entanglement of other animals in the lives of human beings across different

---

[1] Ideas for this paper arose initially from a panel presentation on speciesism presented at the Society for Christian Ethics conference in Chicago, January 2013.

cultures. I argue that such an account illumines the human moral condition, including traditional theological accounts of the origins of morality as expressed in the narrative of the Fall of humanity.

Fourth, I argue that my evolutionary account has ethical implications, including those that press a case for considering other animals through the lens of *inter-morality*. I am not simply claiming that some non-human animals engage the world in ways analogous to human morality. Rather, I am arguing that human moral lives are tied up in highly significant ways with those of other animals. In other words, we become moral not only through our interactions with other humans, but also in relation to a wide diversity of other animals, some of whom act in ways that speak of a morality suited to their worlds. I am not suggesting that morality in other animals is identical to that in humans, nor that all animals express such characteristics, nor even that the behavior characteristic of some other species provides a model for human action. What I am trying to do is find suitable language to describe the complexity and sensitivity of other highly social animal lives in relation to each other and to human beings, language which describes their forms of flourishing as a form of moral agency, though not the same as our own.

Making other animals in our own image is, I suggest, a mistake; but what it not mistaken is viewing how particular other animal social communities and human communities are closely interwoven even in the course of each becoming moral. In order to make a case for that I draw on:

(1) *anthropological studies that seek to clarify differences between human beings Homo sapiens sapiens and other hominins*[2] *in terms of an emerging community niche and niche construction theory*. This section is important as it shifts a discussion of evolutionary theory from one bent on a study of individual creatures that adapt to given environments through the natural selection of particular traits or characteristics to a focus on the significance of community relationships in the process of evolution as such.

(2) *an analysis of relationships between Homo sapiens and other hominin species and their bearing on the doctrines of sin and the Fall of humanity*. Knowledge of good and evil refers to the ability to discriminate, and therefore make sophisticated ethical decisions; but I argue that such capacities do not arise out of the blue.

This observation is significant in so far as it highlights the close relationship with other creatures even in biblical accounts of the

---

[2] Since the terminology in the literature to describe human ancestors is somewhat confusing, note that I am defining "hominin" to mean all modern humans, extinct humans, including members of the genera *Homo, Australopithecus, Paranthropus* and *Ardipithecus*, and defining "hominid" as a broader term, including both more remote human ancestors, one's whose descendants include chimpanzees, gorillas and orangutans..

origin of human awareness of good and evil. The Genesis account of the Fall is, arguably, a grand narrative that sets the scene for the emergence of humans as distinctively moral beings in terms of their culpability. But I suggest that such culpability—and indeed their salvific horizon – does not arise in isolation, but in association with other animals and other living kinds.

(3) *case studies on the entangled evolutionary, ecological and social relationships between the genus Homo and other social species, using hyenas and elephants as examples*.[3]

Finally, I will briefly comment on the way other animals as agential beings and having a type of prudence crop up in the work of medieval theologian Albertus Magnus and his student Thomas Aquinas.

IS HUMAN NATURE SPECIESIST?

The accusation that the Roman Catholic tradition is heavily "speciesist," while becoming less shrill, has led to some sharp counter reactions. The late Polish Archbishop Josef Życiński, for example, heavily criticizes Peter Singer and Tom Regan in the same breath that he is concerned about the demerits of evolutionary accounts of human nature.[4] But the anxieties related to the two trajectories of anti-speciesism and evolutionary theory are different. In the first case of anti-speciesism, expanding human moral concern to include other animal kinds should not, in principle at least, denigrate concern for humans. In Peter Singer's case, weakening of concern for human beings is more a consequence of his approach to moral philosophy, such as his reliance on *sentience* as a key moral criterion, and utilitarian approach to moral reasoning, rather than the fact *per se* that he has admitted that other animal kinds are worthy of moral consideration.[5] The Roman Catholic tradition encourages moving beyond exclusivist and parochial moral concerns to more global perspectives, including that of

---

[3] Among many other fascinating examples is the work by Eduardo Kohn, which shows how the presence of pumas understood as active subjects among the Runa people of the Amazon opens up an anthropology sensitive to signs and indices emerging in other animals, as well as symbolic language representation distinctive of humans. Kohn uses Pierce's semiotic discourse to interpret detailed anthropological studies of Runa. See E. Kohn, *How Forests Think: Towards an Anthropology Beyond the Human* (Berkeley: University of California Press, 2013).

[4] The late Archbishop presupposed that it is necessary to envisage a deep gulf between humans and other species in order to affirm Catholic teaching on distinctive ontological difference between humans and other animals, and human ensoulment though divine intervention. For further discussion of the "gap" mentality see Celia Deane-Drummond, "God's Image and Likeness in Humans and Other Animals: Performative Soul Making and Graced Nature," *Zygon* 47, no. 4 (2012): 1-16.

[5] A much fuller discussion of this topic can be found in Charles Camosy, *Peter Singer and Christian Ethics: Beyond Polarization* (Cambridge: Cambridge University Press, 2012). John Berkman also discusses this on p. 13-14 of his article "From Theological Speciesism to a Theological Ethology" in this issue of the *JMT*.

other animals, even if such strands have not always been sufficiently appreciated.[6] Belief in creation and its value therefore forestalls both strident accusations of speciesism and equally strident counter-reactions.

The second case of suspicion of evolutionary theory as inevitably dangerous for proper consideration of human nature also needs closer inspection. Evolutionary theorists are not, however, the main culprits in resisting strong notions of human nature. "Human nature" is a loaded term in as much as philosophers who favor deconstructive approaches deny the possibility that there can be human nature at all. Biologists may be influenced by such theories in wanting to reject any fixity of nature, though some evolutionary psychologists still rely on a biological definition of humanity as a way of working out what that human nature is like; that is, they associate human nature with the human *species*. There are many different interpretations of what human nature might mean, ranging from a focus on what "kind" human beings are, whether defined by supposed natural or culturally constructed properties, or whether "human nature" is a search for uniqueness and a code for a definition of the human in distinction from other animals.[7] Philosophical premises are significant for what I term evolutionary suspicion, which relates to concern that evolutionary theory cuts out or diminishes any significant moral difference between human beings and other animals, and on that basis undermines particular Roman Catholic concern for the human person. But different evolutionary accounts of human becoming need to be interrogated as far as their *metaphysical* presuppositions are concerned, before ruling out *all* evolutionary accounts as morally dangerous.

Finding positivistic examples of what might be termed naturalistic ethics and a rampant human evolution*ism* is certainly not difficult. Such a view is more often than not associated with a search for a universal human natural "kind" that is then used as a basis for evolutionary *origins* of particular characteristics, some latent forms of which may be present in other animal "kinds." Forms of such evolutionism become particularly striking in the discussion of the evolution of morality and religion by authors such as Richard Joyce and Donald

---

[6] As discussed in many of the other essays in this special issue.

[7] Delving into the philosophical presuppositions behind each possible definition is beyond the scope of this article, but see Jonathan Jong and Aku Visala, "Three Quests for Human Nature: Some Philosophical Presuppositions," *Philosophy, Theology and the Sciences* 1 (2014), *in press.* The authors also characterize a third quest for human nature in terms of "innateness," that itself is subject to a variety of definitions, but tends to focus on those characteristics that are insensitive to environmental influences. All three dominant portraits on human nature that focus on universalism, uniqueness and innateness fail to appreciate properly the dynamic interplay between human beings and other animals that itself has shaped what human beings are like, both in biological and cultural perspectives.

Broom.[8] It is easy to see the problematic aspects of Joyce's discussion, as his positioning of moral concepts in evolutionary terms then leads to his argument for doubting their validity.[9] But this argument is weak, not least because if all concepts are filtered out through an interpretation of natural selection, then such a filter could in theory equally undermine belief in anything at all, even evolutionary science. In addition, scientific confidence in an exclusivist genetic explanation for morality is not nearly as solid as Joyce implies. He seems, therefore, to harbor a narrowly conceived understanding of evolution by natural selection that depends on genetic or "innate" human capacities, rather than a much richer evolutionary account that includes epigenetic, cultural and symbolic inheritance systems.[10] Secondly, even if a case for a neo-Darwinian account can be made, such morality is likely to have been selected for in a way that corresponds with truth claims about reality rather than simply being arbitrary.

Arguments for undermining humanist moral concepts are taken even further in Steve Stewart-Williams, who, while rejecting evolutionary ethics, argues against any concepts of human dignity on the basis that it reflects a pre-Darwinian anthropogenic view of the universe that now has to be rejected.[11] In addition to his more specific argument against human dignity he rejects the possibility that there can be any objective moral truths.[12] But this is a philosophical metanarrative and an example of scient*ism* that does not necessarily have to cohere with evolutionary accounts of human becoming. Further, as I will show below, recognition of the entanglement of different species with our own does not need to align with rejection of human distinctiveness.

---

[8] Richard Joyce, *The Evolution of Morality* (Cambridge: MIT Press, 2006); Donald Broom, *The Evolution of Morality and Religion* (Cambridge: Cambridge University Press, 2003).

[9] Joyce, *Evolution of Morality*, 180-1. He speaks of a "belief pill" that he represents in terms of natural selection, so that if our ancestry has encouraged concepts like obligation, property, virtue and fairness, then we should be skeptical of their positive value without further evidence.

[10] For an alternative approach to evolution, see Eva Jablonka and Marion Lamb, *Evolution in Four Dimensions* (Cambridge: MIT Press, 2005).

[11] Steve Stewart-Williams, *Darwin, God, and the Meaning of Life: How Evolutionary Theory Undermines Everything You Thought You Knew* (Cambridge: Cambridge University Press, 2010).

[12] Given the nihilism that he finds as a logical outcome of evolutionary biology, he rejects beginning with evolutionary biology; instead, he argues we have to decide what we value and then allow evolutionary biology to give guidance. See Stewart-Williams, *Darwin,* 256. But if this is the case, what is presupposed in coming to decide what is of value?

Evolutionary perspectives on the rise of the human

In order to elaborate human distinctiveness further in a way that is *inclusive* rather than exclusive in relation to other animals, I intend to comment on work that is still under development in cultural and social anthropology. Here I will be asking, what are ways in which evolutionary accounts of human becoming *illuminate* theological understanding of human distinctiveness? Further, is there a way of incorporating evolutionary insights without a commitment to a somewhat arbitrary "biologism" that claims so called "natural" properties are foundational for understanding human nature? One way to do this is to see human evolution in anthropological terms through a long trajectory in relationship with other hominins and other species. In this section I will deal with the former. Anthropology has the advantage of being able to engage with both humanities literature and that of the sciences, and is therefore an extremely valuable conversation partner for theologians entering this difficult intellectual terrain. Anthropologists and evolutionary biologists concur that present day humans are not simply a species, *Homo sapiens*, but rather collectively form a sub-species within a species, *Homo sapiens sapiens*. We are *doubly* imbibed with wisdom. But how are we to perceive human becoming in evolutionary terms? Certainly, for a biologist, the categorization of "species" is a way of labeling a large suite of characteristics that served that population group well in terms of its evolutionary success.

In earlier millennia in which the genus *Homo* gradually came to be prominent, there is strong evidence of not just one but many co-existing lineages.[13] For example, some of the archaic hominin species that existed from over four million years ago overlapped with the transitional species of the *Homo* genus, *H.habilis* and *H.rudolfensis*, a little over two million years ago, and these species in turn overlapped in time with *H.ergaster*, one of the so called extant modern hominins that appeared about two million years ago, along with subsequent *Homo* species *H.erectus, H.heidelbergensis, H.neanderthalis, H.antecessor* and *H.florensiensis*. All these *Homo* species, apart from *H.antecessor*, were around when *H.sapiens* appeared, and *H.florensiensis* appeared and disappeared during the period after *H.sapiens* emerged. Of course, all these *Homo* species are defined on the basis of their particular distinguishing marks of anatomy and other visible characteristics that have been left in the anthro-paleo-archeological record. However, a clearer portrait of the lifeworlds of these different *Homo* species and earlier archaic hominins is gradually developing, but there are still considerable areas of scientific uncertainty. Anthropologists are beginning to appreciate that it is not enough just to pick out one charac-

[13] Bernard Wood, "Reconstructing human evolution: achievements, challenges, and opportunities," *Proc Natl Acad Sc*i USA 107 (2010): 8902-9.

teristic as if *that* was the defining moment in marking human speciation. Instead, building on recognition of what can be termed the emergence of super-sociality, it is the evolution of the community *system as a whole* in its ecological, social and neurological dimensions that is relevant, which, in turn impacts on the subsequent historical, psychological, cultural and eventually moral and religious becomings.[14]

The mapping of specific characteristics at each stage shows profound overlap in capacities between different hominins and hominids. Of course, the fascinating question to both anthropologists and theologians is *why* was a particular sub species of the *Homo sapiens* lineage, *Homo sapiens sapiens*, so much more successful compared with other *Homo* groups that co-existed with it? One possible answer is that there was no single trait involved, but a multiplicity of factors that influenced the development of the particular community niche in a particular way. Early hominins also shared strong social reciprocity. In this model, symbol creation appeared relatively late on in evolutionary terms, but cultural innovation permitted positive feedback. To put this more simply, early humans learnt by *doing*, involving a multiplicity of characteristics, otherwise known as the apprentice model, suggested by Kim Sterelny.[15] But the evolutionary puzzle remains as to what allowed one group, *Homo sapiens sapiens* to persist when the other recognizably different groups of modern hominins did not? Although the cultural characterization of *H. neanderthalis*, for example, has often been cast in a negative light, there is some discussion as to how much inter-species overlap with *H.sapiens* took place.[16] The discovery of genetic transfer between the groups implies some cases of interbreeding.[17] Ian Tattersall believes that the excitement over such a discovery is far too premature, and that any gene transfer reflects an occasional "hanky panky" rather than a genuine blurring of community boundaries.[18] Hence, an evolutionary perspective implies some fluidity of boundaries, but distinctions are such to keep communities glued together for the most part. The fact that there was *some* transfer

---

[14] Agustin Fuentes, "The Community Niche as Focal Context in Assessing Pleistocene Human Evolution," *Current Anthropology, in preparation*. I am grateful to Agustin for sharing work in progress. For published work see A. Fuentes, "Humans as Niche Constructors, as Primates, and with Primates: Synergies for Anthropology in the Anthropocene." *Cambridge Anthropology* 30, no. 2 (2012): 140-4.

[15] Kim Sterelny, *The Evolved Apprentice: How Evolution Made Humans Unique* (Boston: MIT Press, 2012).

[16] Stephen Mithen has suggested that Neanderthals communicated by music. See S. Mithen, *The Singing Neanderthals: The Origins of Music, Language, Mind, and Body* (Cambridge: Harvard University Press, 2008).

[17] See Joao Zilhao,"The Emergence of Language, Art and Symbolic Thinking," in *Homo symbolicus: The Dawn of Language, Imagination and Spirituality*, ed. C. N. Henshilwood and F. D'Errico (Amsterdam: John Benjamins, 2011), 111-31.

[18] Ian Tattersall, *Masters of the Planet: The Search for Our Human Origins* (New York: Palgrave MacMillan, 2012).

suggests that the two "species" were cross-fertile, but the fact that this did not happen to any large extent implies geographical and/or cultural separation, as well as the anatomically distinctions that eventually cemented those distinctions.

What is the evolutionary significance of hominin species being understood primarily in the context of a community? The issue here relates to a relatively new emphasis on niche construction theory in a biological understanding of human evolution. Jeremy Kendal *et al.* suggests that "the defining characteristic of niche construction is not the modification of environments per se, but rather the organism-induced changes in selection pressures in environments."[19] Importantly for the present paper, niche construction theory (NCT) represents a philosophical shift in the way evolutionary processes work, so that while some have incorporated aspects of NCT in their frameworks, a more radical approach is to examine evolutionary questions under the umbrella of NCT, rather than simply adding it on to previous dominant models.[20] It is particularly interesting in my view as it provides a significant bridge between the biological sciences and the human, cultural sciences.

A standard theory of evolution is "externalist" in as much as the environment is perceived as external factors that act in order to select those internal properties of individuals and populations that are most adapted to that environment. Natural selection in this view is the "ultimate" category that explains phenotype, including behavioral differences, and therefore devalues more "proximate" causes. Hence, standard evolution theory can still include NCT, but the "ultimate" explanation is still one rooted in natural selection. In the newer approach to NCT, the idea of some sort of direct evolutionary "causation" through natural selection becomes problematized. So the "dichotomous proximate and ultimate distinction" is replaced by "reciprocal causation."[21] In this way, niche construction works *with* natural selection in the evolutionary process in a dynamic interchange. Niches are themselves part of the inheritance process, so that an interactionist evolutionary theory replaces an externalist theory. Niche construction emphasizes

---

[19] Jeremy Kendal, Jamshid J. Tehrani, and F. John Odling-Smee, "Human Niche Construction in Interdisciplinary Focus," *Philosophical Transactions of the Royal Society B* 366 (2011), 785-92.

[20] The mathematical expression of NCT is straightforward. Standard evolutionary theory assumes an organism's state is a function of the organism and the environment (dO/dt=f(O,E) and changes in the environment are a simply a function of that environment (dE/dt=g(E)). NCT, on the other hand, allows for the organism to be able to *change* the environment, and so can be expressed mathematically as dO/dt=f (O,E) and dE/dt=g (O,E).

[21] Kendal *et al,* "Human Niche Construction," 786.

not just genetic, epigenetic and cultural inheritance, but also ecological inheritance as well, in dynamic interaction.[22] But even in this model, envisioning cultural aspects as somehow separate from ecological inheritance seems too constraining. Ecological and cultural inheritance under a broader "ecological" category carries the advantage of perceiving a developmental context in which the physical niche is not separated from the social niche.[23]

The importance of this dynamic interactionist view cannot be overstated. It removes, in the first place, the strong determinism that is often characteristic of evolutionary accounts that rely on purely externalist models. Instead, creatures become agents capable of shaping their own evolution, even if such agency is only perceived to be such by a tiny fraction of creaturely beings, namely *Homo sapiens sapiens*. Augustin Fuentes envisages that in the course of hominin history the community niche gradually shifted.[24] So the suite of communal characteristics found in modern humans are associated with changes that took place in evolutionary history. He envisages that rather than simply using anatomical markers, the function of communities in the evolution of the genus *Homo* allow for four different community niches to be distinguished, namely: 1) early *Homo* (2.3mya – 1.5mya), 2) *Homo erectus* (1.5mya – 0.7mya), 3) *H. erectus*/archaic *Homo* (0.7mya – 0.3mya), 4) modern humans. In this model the earliest *Homo* communities existing more than 1.5 million years ago were small and static and suffered extinctions. Over time these moved eventually to larger, more communicative, interactive and far more flexible groups. Symbolic and cultural innovation in this model appeared prior to the development of full-blown symbolic language in the transition between niche 3 and niche 4.

Fully organized religion did not appear until much later, around 10,000 years ago, so could not account for this transition. However, it seems highly likely that the capability for imagination and what could be termed transcendental thinking, including latent forms of religious experience, appeared very much earlier than first recorded evidence of either early cave paintings or organized religious beliefs. In a fascinating paper Maurice Bloch argues that it is the generalized capacity to envisage transcendental social relationships that distinguishes humans

---

[22] This threefold model of Laland *et al.* compares with the four dimensions of evolution suggested by Jablonka and Lamb. The difference in this case is a greater emphasis on the ecological aspects; the latter allow for niche construction, but place this in the context of behavioral change and symbolic change as two of the four dimensions of evolution. Kevin N. Laland, F. John Odling-Smee, and Marc W. Feldman, "Cultural Niche Construction and Human Evolution," *Behavioral Brain Sciences* 23 (2000): 131-75.

[23] F. John Odling-Smee, "Niche Inheritance," in *Evolution: The Extended Synthesis*, ed. M. Pigliucci and G. B. Muller (Cambridge: MIT Press, 2010), 175-207.

[24] Fuentes, "The Community Niche."

from primate relatives, who are only capable of transactional relationships in the social sphere.[25] The view that there was no single trait of a given *Homo* species that accounted for their success relative to other co-existing groups seems a convincing argument, even if it is difficult in such a complex model to find ways of proving its evolutionary lineage. But the important point to note in the present context is that such a view allows for the evolutionary importance of biological *and* cultural inheritance and community development. And it does so in a way that undercuts the implicit genetic determinism characteristic of externalist models, a determinism that threatens human distinctiveness and is thus offensive to theologians such as Życiński. Yet the latter's stress on human uniqueness and the adherence to a gulf between humans and other creaturely kinds also needs to be challenged further. Human distinctiveness is certainly there, unless a decision is made to dispense entirely with evolutionary science, but that distinctiveness depends on collaborative and active models of the human being, who has, in community contexts, gradually become more successful in shaping its own destiny.

EVOLUTIONARY PERSPECTIVES ON MORALITY AND THE FALL

In the light of the above evolutionary argument against an account of human uniqueness premised on a gulf between humans and other animals, and the revision in evolutionary theory that takes much more account of a dynamic portrait of human beings embedded in their social communities, what is the meaning of the doctrines of original sin and the Fall of humanity? Should they be flatly rejected as outmoded and unhelpful for illuminating the human condition?[26] If the Fall is understood as a simple spreading of destructive behavior, then there is ample evidence to suggest that communities learned by imitation of others in a way that was passed down from one community to the next, and thus need not depend on language as such. The evolutionary record also suggests that over time when communities became much larger they also became more violent. But the Fall narrative in Genesis seems to mean more than this, namely, a deliberate turning away from God and a prideful assertion of self as God, *sicut deus*, in its place.

[25] His extension of this argument as an explanatory tool for religious belief is more sophisticated than some variants of the same argument, but still falls short of understanding the impact of religious belief on human societies. In other words, he ignores the possibility of revelatory experience. See Maurice Bloch, "Why Religion is Nothing Special but is Central" *Philosophical Transactions of The Royal Society B: Biological Sciences* 363, no. 1499 (2008): 2055-61.

[26] John Mahoney has taken this step by rejecting the traditions of original sin and the Fall in his *Christianity and Evolution* (Washington: Georgetown University Press, 2011), 51-59, 71-97. Unfortunately he is still strongly wedded to an externalist view of evolution, so misses the subtlety that alternative evolutionary models now provide in relation to more traditional interpretations of sin and the Fall. He also fails to criticize the scientism implicit in much evolutionary psychology.

Some evolutionary biologists have tried to account for the emergence of religion through what might be called an "original sin" model, where those who fail to cooperate in a community ("sinners") are in need of punishment, and therefore God is invented by that community in order to provide a convenient and very cost effective way of dealing with that difficulty.[27] In this case, the temptation to do wrong against others in a community comes first, what is known in evolutionary game theory parlance as "free riders," and then religious belief follows in order to suppress that tendency. The traditional Genesis account of the Fall of the first human pair inverts this view entirely and argues that the relationship with God is primary and that the possibility of right relationship with God is realized in the Garden of Eden. God is not an "agent" like other creaturely agents, but the presence of the divine in all that is. The conscious communication of human beings with God marks the dawn of human religious experience.

Classic Catholic theological accounts of the Fall of humanity require some radical revision if they are to be tenable, because they tend to assume some sort of biological inheritance of Adam's guilt, which Augustine believed was transmitted through the semen.[28] Ironically, perhaps, biology is taken far too seriously in this account of original sin. Possibly the most instructive use of biology in a contemporary interpretation is to draw on psychology in the way that Kierkegaard attempted, so that at the root of original sin there is an existential anxiety that then becomes part of every subsequent free decision.[29] Karl Rahner, on the other hand, favors a socially mediated interpretation and argued that original sin refers to that situation of guilt *into* which every human decision is then made.[30] It is important to distinguish between original sin understood as an ontological condition in which human beings find themselves, and moral sin as those acts that a human being is held to account. The latter takes place in the context of the former, but viewed in this way this avoids either the imputation of guilt on neonates or an adherence to a historically literal Garden of Eden, Adam and Eve.

---

[27] Dominic Johnson, "Why God is the Best Punisher," *Religion, Brain and Behavior* 1, no. 1 (2011): 77-84.

[28] Augustine, *The City of God*, Bk. XIV, www.newadvent.org/fathers/-120114.htm. Elaine Pagels is one of many scholars castigating such a view of the origin of sin as "absurd." Elaine Pagels, *Adam, Eve and the Serpent* (London: Weidenfeld and Nicholson, 1988), 109.

[29] Soren Kierkegaard, *The Concept of Anxiety: A Simple Psychologically Orientating Deliberation on the Dogmatic Issue of Hereditary Sin,* ed. Reidar Thornte and Albert B. Anderson (Princeton: Princeton University Press, 1980).

[30] Karl Rahner, "Original Sin," in *Sacramentum Mundi: An Encyclopedia of Theology Vol. 4*, ed. Karl Rahner (London: Burns and Oates, 1969), 328-34.

My own view is that the significance of Adam and Eve is historical, but without implying literal figures. Death is not so much the introduction of mortality, which would make no sense in evolutionary terms, but the absence of flourishing. This fits in with biblical interpretations of Adam, as from the earth, and Eve, the source of life, where both figures stand for the beginnings of the human race and what it might have become, while taking "immortality" as figurative of a flourishing life rather than literal death. In this sense, evolutionary history is still relevant, but without needing to posit a literal pair through which evolution took its course, which is of course extremely difficult to square with evolutionary science.[31]

The active presence of another animal agent in the story of the Fall, namely, *the snake*, even if this is also considered mythological and pre-historical, is also fascinating to reflect on further in the context of this article. Richard Middleton argues that the best translation of the term in the Hebrew text of Genesis is actually *snake*, rather than serpent, thus implying the active involvement of another creature created by God, rather than simply a mythological rendition of evil in the form of another kind.[32] The snake in the biblical text (Gen. 3.1) is simply one of the wild animals that God had made, and by implication was not domesticated in any way, yet was still named and therefore recognized in some way by Adam. From a biological perspective fear of snakes seems to be deeply rooted in evolutionary terms,[33] so associating a particular snake with misfortune makes sense in as much as it is allied with a real threat to human life. At the same time, the biblical text certainly does not imply that the snake was intrinsically evil, but rather "crafty" (*'ārûm*), translated elsewhere as subtle, cunning, shrewd and even intelligent.[34] What is really fascinating is that such intelligence is also occasionally associated in the wisdom literature with the capacity for prudence. Yet, such capacity is not so much a moral *virtue*, but rather implying an innate smartness that could be used for gain and either good or evil ends. The narrative about the snake in the biblical text hints at a moral agency that could be used positively or negatively, so the snake is morally ambiguous. It was

---

[31] There is insufficient space to discuss this in detail, but I take it up in C. Deane-Drummond, "In Adam All Die? Questions at the Boundary of Niche Construction, Community Evolution and Original Sin," work in progress for book volume on Evolution and the Fall, edited by William Cavanaugh and Jamie Smith.

[32] Richard Middleton, "Reading Genesis 3 Attentive to Human Evolution: Beyond Concordism and Non-Overlapping Magisteria", work in progress for book volume on Evolution and the Fall, edited by William Cavanaugh and Jamie Smith.

[33] For a discussion of human association with snakes see the chapter on "The Serpent" in the influential book by E. O. Wilson, *Biophilia: The Human Bond with Other Species* (Cambridge: Harvard University Press, 1984); 83-100.

[34] Middleton, "Reading Genesis 3", in preparation.

through interactions with the human couple that self-conscious capacity for moral choice emerged. Prior to that encounter the couple were largely innocent and ignorant.

How might original sin be interpreted in the light of NCT?[35] In classic interpretations of the Genesis text Adam and Eve are viewed as an isolated dyad, a pair that has resonated in literary and cultural history.[36] If such a view is taken as a literal historical portrait it becomes virtually impossible to square with modern evolutionary biology. Secular anthropology has also moved away from perceiving early hominins in terms of the isolated pair bond, to a much greater sense of the collective. Early *Homo* groups certainly seemed to be highly cooperative, and mass violence was relatively rare, appearing later in the history of our species as the size of community groups exploded. However, it is perhaps forcing the account to associate the early pre-violent condition of *Homo sapiens* with any "paradisiacal" state. What is interesting, none the less, is that the earliest account in the Genesis text associates paradise with harmonious relationships with other co-specifics and other creaturely kinds in a way that at least coheres with the perception of the lifeworlds of the earliest modern *Homo sapiens* species as entangled with each other and other species and in small supportive cooperative communities. Further, in as much as verbal communication apparently took place between God and these early human beings, some language must have been possible, which confines the account to community niche four, and thus to *Homo sapiens,* and most likely to *Homo sapiens sapiens.* It is therefore possible to align aspects of traditional interpretations of the biblical text with contemporary evolutionary theory, even while recognizing that all evolutionary and biological accounts have their limitations in as much as they are based on particular and perhaps peculiarly modern interpretations of what human beings are like. The objection that the Genesis text is not intended to be either a historical or a biological account of origins holds to the extent that the language used in Genesis is mythological rather than literal, but I suggest that an interpretation of such texts against a backcloth of contemporary knowledge of human becoming is nonetheless still illuminating.

---

[35] I am leaving aside for the moment the question as to whether it is theologically justifiable to have any notion of original sin; what I am interested in here is the influence that original sin has had on human perception and the biological preoccupation of its earliest protagonists.

[36] For an interpretive survey of such literature see Brian Murdoch, *Adam's Grace: Fall and Redemption in Medieval Literature* (Cambridge: D.S. Brewer, 2000).

INTER-SPECIES AND INTER-MORALITY: ELEPHANTS AND HYENAS AS CASE STUDIES

So far I have argued that human distinctiveness needs to be situated in the context of a nuanced account of evolutionary theory that recognizes sufficiently the importance of community relationships. Human beings become human and become moral through these relationships. But for the bulk of human history that association has not been done alone, but in association with other hominin kinds that co-existed with our own species. Further, biologists recognize that species labels are really markers for broad shifts in kind, rather than implying a fixity or lack of fluidity. Significant amounts of Neanderthal genetic material have become deeply embedded in the *Homo sapiens* lineage and persists to this day. The Biblical record of the Fall of humanity can, I have argued, be squared with evolutionary accounts of human origins if death is associated with a lack of flourishing. These ancient accounts of moral origins also spell out the significance of a particular wild animal, the snake, at the dawn of moral awareness in humans. Finally and crucially it is important to consider the significance of inter-relationships between *Homo sapiens* and not just other hominins, but other social animals as well. This is important as it shows how morality emerges in association with animal kinds, including the Genesis account of the Fall discussed above.

The argument I have made for a strong community understanding of human becoming and being, including a religious turn and internalization of that in sinful self-idolatry, does not mean that the community was closed or not actively interacting with its environment. Indeed, the definition of community niche is one that *includes* an active ecological dimension. Can we go further than this and ask about the possibility of significant social interaction not just between hominins, but between phylogenetically unrelated species? For this I am going to explore two sets of relationships based on field research and historical studies, that between humans and elephants, and that between humans and hyenas.[37] I use these hyenas and elephants as they are social beings, unlike the snake referred to in the biblical account, even though, arguably, human relationships with snakes are also highly significant, but in a way that does not present snakes as having any kind of capacity for an implicit moral world, since they are reptiles rather than social mammals. Elephants have a long history of association with humans, representing weapons of war, prestige, even symbols of divinity, entertainment, icons of conservation, vehicles for labor, as well as companion animals. As Piers Locke suggests, elephants are "caught up in human enterprises of power, wealth, worship, pleasure

---

[37] I have discussed the latter in more detail in C. Deane-Drummond, *The Wisdom of the Liminal: Human Nature, Evolution and Other Animals* (Grand Rapids: Eerdmans, 2014), *in press*.

and preservation. Feared or worshipped, killed or conserved, captured or maimed, appropriated for stories and symbols, they are animals with whom humanity is profoundly entangled."[38] The hyena association with humans is even more surprising as they are culturally associated with death and destruction.

Locke's review of current literature shows the extent to which elephants are capable of learning, retaining and transmitting practical skills and social information. Perhaps most poignant of all, it is the individual personalities of elephants that are capable of influencing patterns of interaction according to social convention. So they can recognize each other as individuals as well as:

> appreciate the thoughts and feelings of other sentient beings and engage in strategic behavior. Like humans elephants have a high encephalization quotient (brain/body weight ratio), a highly developed neocortex and a high neuron density, all of which are associated with complex learning skills and behaviors. Finally, like humans, elephants grieve for lost friends and relatives.[39]

Locke proposes, therefore, that a research program called ethnoelephantology be adopted that is characterized by three principles: 1) subjective agency of both humans and elephants, i.e. both have sentient and affective lifeworlds, 2) coevolution of humans and elephants in their mutually entangled social, historical and ecological relationships, and, 3) bio-cultural methodology that draws on both the natural and social sciences.[40]

From an interdisciplinary approach there follows an ethical approach towards elephants that puts greater stress on coexistence.[41] However, I wish to go further in this article and argue for an intersected "inter-morality," that is, human morality that is informed and shaped by a form of morality in so far as it exists in other co-evolved social species. The point is that understanding both who we are as humans and more specifically human morality as it has emerged in the human community does not make sense if it is conceived of in isolation from other species and their actions and reactions with humans and other beings. The incentive for such a shift comes not simply from

---

[38] Piers Locke, "Explorations in Ethnoelephantology: Social, Historical, and Ecological Intersections Between Asian Elephants and Humans," *Environment and Society: Advances in Research* 4 (2013): 80.

[39] Locke, "Explorations in Ethnoelephantology," 79-80.

[40] Locke, "Explorations in Ethnoelephantology," 80. Similar arguments have been made for developing ethnoprimatology in Agustin Fuentes, "Naturalcultural Encounters in Bali: Monkeys, Temples, Tourists, and Ethnoprimatology," *Cultural Anthropology* 25 no. 4 (Nov 2010): 600-624.

[41] Christen Wemmer and Catherine Christen, ed., *Elephants and Ethics: Toward a Morality of Coexistence* (Baltimore: John Hopkins University Press, 2008).

bio-cultural studies, but also post-humanism that puts a greater emphasis on recognizing the significance of animal as well as human becomings in mutually entangled ways.[42]

Such a perspective on inter-morality also follows from the work of Michael Hathaway, who applies actor network theory (ANT) used in human geography to the relationships between elephants and the social and natural landscapes of Xishuanbanna in southern Yunnan.[43] So, elephants play a significant, albeit unequal role in the network of interrelationships that link up scientists, government officials, farmers, conservationists and tourists, especially those that deal with elephant-human conflict, species survival and animal welfare. The point is that human decision making about how to act morally in this context is also dependent on how elephants themselves act, including more destructive habits such as colliding with cars or destroying houses. Locals claim that elephants' protected status has led to the elephants changing their habits and exploiting their greater freedom, but then the counter reaction to elephant destructive behavior that includes discourses on indigenous rights brings in a new moral dimension. Of course, I am not for a moment suggesting that the elephants have a pre-conceived or even deliberative sense in their actions and relations to humans. Instead, to the extent that elephants are able to strategize and act collectively, and thus express forms of social relationship, in those geographical regions where they live in close proximity with human beings, such complex behavior also impinges heavily on the human sphere and the particular ethical status that elephants enjoy in that entangled community.

The position I am advocating edges towards a view of elephants as non-human persons, as recommended by a number of anthropologists currently working in this field.[44] Charles Camosy is also prepared to use the moral category of personhood to describe agency in other animals.[45] Of course, such labeling depends on what personhood means, which in Camosy's case seems to equate with divine image bearing. I am rather more reluctant to use such a label, not because I do not recognize agency in other animals, and what can be described their indi-

---

[42] Donna Haraway's work on naturecultures, a rejection of human exceptionalism and her acknowledgement of inter-species dependencies provides the background to this discussion. See, for example, Donna Haraway, *When Species Meet* (Minneapolis: University of Minnesota Press, 2008).

[43] Michael Hathaway, "On the Backs of Elephants: Transnational Environmentalism and Elephant Agency," in Hathaway, *Environmental Winds: Making the Global in Southwest China* (Berkeley: University of California Press, 2013), 152-184.

[44] Locke cites Ursula Münster and Nurit Bird-David and Danny Naveh in this respect. See Locke, "Explorations in Ethnoelephantology," 86.

[45] C. Camosy, "Other Animals as Persons," *Animals as Religious Subjects: Transdisciplinary Perspectives*, ed. C. Deane-Drummond, D. Clough & R. Artinian-Kaiser (London: Bloomsbury T & T Clark, 2013), 259-78.

viduality and at a stretch, "personality," but because there is a definitive imaginative leap in *Homo sapiens sapiens* that seems to be missing in other animals, including other hominins, for all their sophistication and entanglement in human societies. The point I am arguing here is not that other animals are equivalent to humans in moral terms, but rather that human morality is shaped by and formed in relationship with other social animals, of which elephants are an excellent example. Further, our capacity for pride and therefore the conscious Fall into sin is one that sits heavy on the human social meshwork of relationships in a way that is highly distinctive of the human condition. At the same time, I want to concede that all animals, especially social animals, show forth both the likeness of God and the tendency for ill in a way that humans can appreciate and recognize.[46]

Locke also draws on his own field experience to show an ontological understanding of elephants by their Nepalese handlers (*hattisare*) variously portrayed as animals, persons and even gods, thus coexisting in diverse relations of dominance, companionship and veneration.[47] Locke argues for companionship, and I would strongly agree with that assessment, without necessarily attributing the term personhood to such relations in the way that he prefers.

The second case study raises equally interesting issues for a consideration of inter-morality, not least because hyenas have commonly been associated with "sin and death" and other negative attitudes in human communities. This association is related to the feeding habits of hyenas, in that they consume all bodies, including the bodies of the dead. Albert the Great comments on hyenas in his monumental *Summa zoologica* on animals:

> The hyena is an animal about the size of a wolf which often inhabits the sepulchers of the dead. It also gladly frequents horse stables. It learns from frequent listening and calls people and dogs by name. It kills the ones it has fooled by calling them and devours them. Sometimes it also deceives people with a wretching sound of vomit. It is said that hunting dogs that come in contact with its shadow lose their bark.[48]

---

[46] See C. Deane-Drummond, "In God's Image and Likeness: From Reason to Revelation in Humans and Other Animals" in *Questioning the Human: Perspectives on Theological Anthropology for the 21st Century*, ed. Lieven Boeve, Yves De Maeseneer & Ellen Van Stichel (New York: Fordham University Press, 2014), *in press.*

[47] Locke, "Explorations in Ethnoelephantology," 87.

[48] Albert continues further: "It is also said that it can change its color at will. Some also say that every animal which crosses its path sticks to its tracks. Jewelers also relate that this beast bears a precious gem in its eyes, or to be more accurate, in its forehead. The hairs on the neck of this animal are like those of a horses mane. Some same its vertebrae are so rigid that it cannot bend its neck without twisting its entire body. Jorach also says that it is sometimes male and sometimes female and that it collects poison on its tail. But this Jorach often lies." Albertus Magnus, *On Animals:*

Now while some of this reflects second hand knowledge and prejudicial attitudes about hyenas that eventually filtered into bestiaries, Albert was unusual as a philosopher and theologian in actively seeking first hand experience of the animals under discussion. Notice that he seems quite prepared to attribute agency to hyenas, even if this is cast in a largely negative light. It is also significant that he was the teacher of Thomas Aquinas.[49]

Given the era in which Albertus Magnus wrote, his remarks about the capabilities of other animals and human distinctiveness sound remarkably modern. For example, "one of the characteristics by which the human is human is the capacity for being ashamed of an ill-done deed. This belongs to no other animal save the human.... [I]ncorrigible people are said to be called shameless, because to some degree they have been changed, moving from the honor of reason to assume an irrational or cattle-like nature."[50] Now while the emotion of shame may or may not be characteristic of other animals, the development of reason understood as not simply intelligence but a self-reflective view on a wrong deed is characteristic of human beings. As indicated in the passage on hyenas noted above, he also recognized that other animals had desires and ends that they pursued, which contrasts with later more wooden interpretations of them as lacking in sensation. So he argued that "it is a strictly human quality to pursue the honorable, whereas all brutes pursue what is useful and pleasurable."[51]

He also set in place the framework for a particular kind of human approach to vice and virtue that is capable of self-reflection, so according to Albert "it is also a strictly human trait to set his passions in order in accordance with virtue and to hold to the limit of reason those things which move in sensation."[52] Even more remarkable, perhaps, he admitted to a form of friendship as possible among other animals, even if he hesitated to attribute to them inter-specific alliances, so: "Likewise, although animals may be friendly among themselves, they only have the appearance of friendship... similar to the one which the

A Medieval Summa Zoologica, trans. K. F. Kitchell and I. M. Resnick (Baltimore: The John Hopkins University Press, 1999), b. 22, ch. 5.

[49] Space does not permit discussion of this here, but several commentators have noted that the hasty castigation of Thomas Aquinas as having an inevitably negative influence on human relationships with other animals is premature. See for example, essays by John Berkman and Celia Deane-Drummond in *Creaturely Theology: On God, Humans and Other Animals*, ed. C. Deane-Drummond and D. Clough (London: SCM Press, 2009).

[50] Albertus Magnus *On Animals,* 22.5.§11.

[51] Albertus Magnus *On Animals,* 22.5.§11.

[52] Albertus Magnus *On Animals,* 22.5.§11.

Greeks call *ethayrica*, this being friendship that stems from the pleasure held by those who have been fed or nursed together. The human, however, possesses every conceivable type of friendship."[53]

The distinctive ability of human beings to generate abstract theories and take pleasure in them sounds remarkably like contemporary discussions of humans as a symbolic species, so he claims that:

> Only the human has the power of speculation on intellectual theorems and being delighted by a pleasurable thing that has no contrary.... It is also proper to the human to be able to learn by the use of his reason, to be gentle by nature due to his civilized character, and to be an animal that can laugh and exult due to the perfect causes of rejoicing that are found only in the human.[54]

Thomas Aquinas took up such threads in his works, and was quite prepared to admit to a form of moral agency in other animals that he named as a type of prudence. For Thomas, "full practical wisdom or prudence is discovered in a person who has sound judgment about how things should be done, while a partial reflection of this is exhibited by some animals whose particular instructive manifestations adapt them to tasks similar to those which tax human ingenuity."[55] So, the seeds of the idea of morality in other creaturely kinds are latent in the Catholic tradition, even if they have not usually been appreciated.

To jump to what is now emerging in a contemporary context is illuminating, as it seems that social history has forgotten the kind of close relationships that Albert recognized. So, Marcus Baynes-Rock investigates the relationship between hyenas and humans through a narrative ethology in the Muslim town of Harar, Ethiopia.[56] He does not name this *ethnohyenatology*, but it follows in a similar vein to the work of Locke discussed above. His observations led Baynes-Rock to conclude that hyenas who lived in the town were not just tolerated by the human population, but were dependent on foods given to them by the human population in order to survive. The lives of both humans and hyenas are intricately linked, extending even to religious practices, so reflecting something of the ambiguity noted by Locke among

---

[53] Albertus Magnus *On Animals*, 22.5.§11.

[54] Albertus Magnus *On Animals*, 22.5.§12.

[55] Thomas Aquinas, *Summa Theologiae*, trans. Fathers of the English Dominican Province (New York: Benziger, 1947), I-II q. 3, a. 6. For a fuller discussion of Aquinas's understanding of prudence in other animals, see Deane-Drummond, *The Wisdom of the Liminal in press*

[56] Marcus Baynes-Rock, *Hyenas Like Us: Social Relations with an Urban Carnivore in Harar, Ethiopia*, PhD thesis (Department of Anthropology, Macquarie University, Australia, 2012). I am grateful to Agustin Fuentes for pointing me to Marcus Baynes-Rock's work and to Marcus Baynes-Rock for permission to draw on his, as yet, unpublished thesis.

hattisare. Even as far back as 4.4 million years ago there was an association between hyenas and *Ardipithecines*, so much so that if hyenas had not been present many more remains would have been discovered. But half a million years later, the hominin *Australopithecus anamensis* is still associated with hyena remains. Likewise, 3.6 million years ago further evidence for such association continues. But the damaged bones of our earliest ancestors had previously been interpreted as evidence for a violent hominin, a "killer ape," persisting in the literature for three decades. Instead, close examination of the bones revealed such hominins were not killer apes at all, but falling prey to carnivores, and the most likely culprits were leopards and hyenas.

The point is that human beings have been associated with hyenas for as long as their history permits, and it is only relatively recently that hyena distribution has become constricted. *Homo ergaster*, *Megantereon whitei* and *Pachycrocuta brevirostris* (giant hyenas almost as tall as the hominins themselves) co-evolved, eventually by 0.5 million years ago being replaced by spotted hyenas, the only African species persisting in Europe after glacial cycles were hyenas and humans, finally disappearing from Europe and Asia a little before ten thousand years ago.[57] Why is this so crucial? I suggest it is crucial because human becoming, including the making of human moral life, has not happened in isolation from other species, but in co-evolutionary contexts. Further, human identity has drawn on millennia of co-existence with other species and millennia of becoming from other related hominin kinds. This account is significant in as much as it challenges narrowly conceived perceptions of the human as being most human in isolation from and in sharp separation from other species. Rather, these companions on our way have helped to shape and re-shape human communities and their moral life, alongside those communities of other animals. And if the work of Baynes-Rock is taken seriously, then the behavior and what we could call a crypto-morality found among hyenas can be modified by their contact with human populations.[58] Hence, as with the case of elephants, we arrive at a kind of inter-morality emerging from an understanding of the inter-specific dynamics of human and other animal relationships.

Conclusions

I began this paper by pointing out that reactions to the charge of "speciesism" in the Catholic tradition have been defensive and exhibit an unwarranted human exceptionalism. Human dignity is not weakened by acknowledging that the boundaries between humans and other animals are much more fluid than presupposed in Western post-Enlightenment societies. Human evolutionary accounts do need to be

---

[57] Marcus Baynes-Rock, *Hyenas Like Us*, 33.

[58] See Deane-Drummond, *The Wisdom of the Liminal, in press.*

scrutinized for their philosophical presuppositions and over-extension in explanatory terms, but at the same time facets of the evolutionary story are highly illuminating for understanding the human condition. In particular, niche construction theory allows greater recognition of the importance of the social in evolutionary accounts, thus rejecting a purely externalist account of evolution by natural selection. Such an opening up appreciates agency in humans and other animals as having a significant impact on evolutionary history. Moreover, the community niche constructed by human beings is one that is entangled with the lives of other species in a dynamic inter-species exchange. The precise reasons why one sub species of hominin was successful when others were not is not yet known, but a reasonable hypothesis is that such early human beings were capable of constructing imaginative transcendental social worlds. In theological terms those worlds allowed for a fuller revelation of the divine to human societies. A distinctive morality in human societies coalesced with a religious sense, so that there was a greater awareness of wrong-doing and according to the biblical record a deliberate Fall into sin. Yet such a Fall of humanity was not done in isolation, either as a pair or as a human community, but rather in relation to other creatures. I then build on current evidence for inter-species sociality in order to make a stronger case for what I have termed *inter-morality*, that is, morality emerging in the human sphere in a way that is shaped by forms of morality that are characteristic of other animal agents. For this, I draw on current work on elephant-human associations, which, like work on allo-primates, shows that humans' life worlds are closely entangled with that of other creatures. Such a view of agency and entanglement is also hinted at in medieval Christian works such as that by Albert the Great. His writing on hyenas was limited by a lack of scientific knowledge of hyenas, which has shown up the length of co-evolution with human beings; in fact hyenas have been associated with humans as far back as the very earliest hominin ancestors. The shaping of religious and moral practices of the people of Harar in Ethiopia illustrates the close nexus between other animals and human societies. In a sense, human becoming and human morality is dependent on the presence of other social creatures with whom humans have associated for millennia. Like Locke, companionship is perhaps the ethical goal of human-other animal relationships, but that goal is one that is also anticipated in Christian eschatology. M

Journal of Moral Theology, Vol. 3, No. 2 (2014): 93-108

Moral Passions: A Thomistic Interpretation of Moral Emotions in Nonhuman and Human Animals

Jean Porter

WHILE WE HAVE A GREAT DEAL IN COMMON with nonhuman animals, we have long assumed that morality is a distinctively human phenomenon. However, a growing body of research into animal behavior suggests that this particular contrast is at best an over-simplification, or even a mistake.[1] Although it can be difficult to interpret the behaviors of nonhuman animals, it does seem fairly clear that social animals of all kinds are capable of empathy, gratitude, indignation, and other similar responses to the behaviors of others. These kinds of emotions are expressed through a range of well-documented behaviors, including comforting those in distress, engaging in reciprocal favors such as grooming or sharing food, refusing to participate in uneven exchanges or even retaliating for disadvantageous treatment. Unless we are prepared to maintain a deep skepticism about the emotions of nonhuman animals, it is difficult to deny that they experience the kinds of feelings about others that we commonly identify as moral emotions.

The question is whether these and similar sensibilities and behaviors should count as morality. According to the distinguished primatologist Frans de Waal, there is at the very least an essential continuity between the relevant responses of nonhumans and human morality. In their introduction to his Tanner Lecture, "Primates and Philosophers," Josiah Ober and Stephen Macedo offer a helpful summary: "Emotional responses are, de Waal argues, the 'building blocks' of human morality. Human moral behavior is considerably more elaborate than that of any nonhuman animal, but in de Waal's view, it is *continuous with* nonhuman behavior.... Given this continuity of good nature,

---

[1] There is by now a considerable body of research supporting this general claim, although of course it remains controversial. For an extended account of de Waal's own pioneering work in this field, see his *Good Natured: The Origins of Right and Wrong in Human and Other Animals* (Cambridge, MA: Harvard University Press, 1996). De Waal and Sarah F. Brosnan offer a comprehensive overview of work in this area, together with suggestions for future research, in "Fairness in Animals: Where to from Here?" *Social Justice Research* 25 (2011): 336-51.

there is no need to imagine morality being mysteriously added to an immoral core"[2]

Most scientists and philosophers today would agree that nonhumans and humans share a great deal that is relevant to morality, including basic moral emotions and corresponding behaviors. Nonetheless, not everyone would agree that nonhuman social behaviors and human morality are essentially two points on a continuum. There are some key elements of human morality that apparently are not found among nonhumans. So far as we can determine, the moral emotions and their corresponding behaviors appear to be elicited only by those within an animal's immediate circle—they do not appear to generalize these responses to include all their co-specifics. Similarly, they do not seem to have a general notion of obligation that would in some way incorporate the more particular kinds of responses into one generalized pattern of action.[3] Again, there appears to be little disagreement about the existence of these discontinuities—the question is, should they count as essential discontinuities, which reflect a distinctively new element in human morality?

It will be apparent by now that this debate, even though it is occasioned by contemporary scientific research, continues a much older debate over the place of reason in morality. De Waal claims that there are no essential differences between human morality and nonhuman moral emotions and their corresponding behaviors, in part because he believes that human morality is fundamentally grounded in emotional responses rather than rational deliberation: "People can deliberate as much as they want, but, as neuroscientists have found, if there are no emotions attached to the various options in front of them, they will never reach a decision or conviction. This is critical for moral choice, because if anything morality involves strong convictions. These convictions don't—or rather can't—come about through a cool rationality: They require caring about others and powerful 'gut feelings' about

---

[2] Frans de Waal and respondents, *Primates and Philosophers: How Morality Evolved*, ed. Stephen Macedo and Josiah Ober (Princeton: Princeton University Press, 2006), xiv, emphasis in the original.

[3] As Ober and Macedo observe, the former issue is raised in some form by all of de Waal's respondents: "Each commentator asks a similar question: If even the most advanced nonhuman animals ordinarily limit their good behavior to insiders (kin or community members) can we really speak of their behavior as *moral*?" *Primates and Philosophers*, xv. Among these respondents, Christine Korsgaard emphasizes the latter issue; see "Morality and the Distinctiveness of Human Action," 98-119 in *Primates and Philosophers*, 116-17. Christopher Boehm observes that while nonhuman animals apparently internalize social norms and associate the violation of these with the threat of punishment, they do not appear to experience self-referential moral emotions with respect to these norms – that is to say, they do not seem to experience guilt or shame. See *Moral Origins: The Evolution of Virtue, Altruism, and Shame* (New York: Basic Books, 2012), 116-31.

right and wrong."[4] Given this overall perspective, de Waal naturally gives little weight to the apparent absence of any sense of universal concern or obligation among nonhuman animals, because these presuppose rational capacities for generalization and abstraction. By the same token, those whose conception of morality gives a central place to rationality will regard the emergence of a sense of universal duty as a watershed, marking a fundamental discontinuity between other kinds of animals and ourselves. On this view, moral judgments presuppose capacities for abstraction and the self-conscious use of general concepts and inferential principles, capacities that so far as we know are distinctively and characteristically human.

For my own part, I side with those who understand morality to be a distinctively rational, and therefore distinctively human phenomenon.[5] Nonetheless, I also agree with de Waal that moral emotions such as sympathy and indignation play a central role in human morality, analogous to—although not essentially similar to—the role they play in nonhuman responses and behaviors. De Waal is right to remind us that we are animals ourselves and share a great deal with other kinds of animals in the structures and processes of our operations as conscious creatures. He challenges those of us who would nonetheless mark discontinuities to interpret these in such a way as to do justice to the real continuities between ourselves and other sentient creatures. This should be a welcome challenge for all of us, because what it really represents is an invitation to think more carefully about the ways in which reasoned judgment and affective response work together in our lives as moral agents.

In this article, I want to address this challenge through an analysis of the moral emotions as inclinations of moral passions, understood in accordance with the moral psychology developed by Thomas Aquinas. I realize that this may appear to be an unpromising approach to a contemporary debate. Aquinas is generally regarded as one of those who emphasizes the central role of reason in human life, and correlatively, the deep discontinuities between men and women on the one hand, and nonhuman animals on the other. But as I hope to show, Aquinas's analysis of the passions and their complex relations to perception, activity, and (among humans) judgment and action offers an illuminating framework for making sense of what we know about the moral emotions in both ourselves and other kinds of animals. On this account, the passions and their corresponding emotions do indeed play a central and necessary role in shaping our perceptions, volitions, and

---

[4] *Primates and Philosophers*, 18.

[5] In this article, I presuppose a Thomistic account of human nature, according to which capacities for rational judgment and desire are characteristic of the form of life proper to men and women as such. For a fuller account and defense of this view, see *Nature as Reason: A Thomistic Theory of the Natural Law* (Grand Rapids: Eerdmans, 2005), 82-124.

choices (*Summa Theologiae* I-II q. 9, a. 2; q. 10, a. 3). They cannot provide an adequate basis for human morality, but nonetheless, our moral lives would literally be unthinkable without them.

In what follows, I develop these claims in two stages. In the first part, I will look more closely at Aquinas's comparative analysis of the passions of nonhuman animals and humans, focusing on the relationship between the passions and perceptions, on the one hand, and self-motion, or goal directed activity, on the other. Aquinas does identify one passion which clearly corresponds to a moral emotion, namely the passion of anger, but in what follows I will focus on his treatment of the passions as such, arguing that everything that Aquinas says about the passions generally applies to what we might call the moral passions (*ST* I-II q. 23, a. 4; I-II q. 46). Secondly, I will look at Aquinas's argument that human passions require some degree of rational formation in order to function at all. Again, this is true for our moral passions, as much as any others, and the rational formation of the moral passions enables the agent to feel and respond in accordance with reasoned judgments of some kind, even without deliberating at every turn. At the same time, Aquinas also apparently believes that the needed rational principles cannot be elicited from perceptions and passions alone—they will necessarily include general rational principles which could not originate at this level, and which are themselves the starting points for a distinctively human kind of appetite, namely the will.

Human and nonhuman animals share much in common, more than we realized until very recently, and we have a great deal to learn about both ourselves and our fellow creatures by reflecting on these commonalities. In this article, I will be asking what a comparison between human and nonhuman forms of moral responsiveness can tell us about ourselves, and I will not attempt to address the related question of what these comparisons imply about nonhuman animals and our relations to them. But at the very least, I hope to show that our lives as moral agents reflect deep continuities, as well as discontinuities, with the ways of life characteristic of many other kinds of animals. To the extent that we take these continuities seriously, we cannot fail to look at nonhuman animals in a different way, not as mechanisms or objects, but as subjects of an inner life similar in some ways to our own. This way of looking at other kinds of animals does not, in itself, prescribe a specific way of relating to them, but it does at least serve to open up relevant questions, and to give them an urgency they might not otherwise have.

In order to prevent confusion or misunderstanding, let me add two further preliminary points. First, as we will see, Aquinas distinguishes between the passions and the inclinations of desire or aversion which stem from those passions. Generally speaking, these inclinations would be equivalent to the emotions, understood as feelings of desire, aversion, or some complex blend of the two. I accordingly distinguish between moral passions and moral emotions, understanding the latter as inclinations stemming from passions of a certain kind. Secondly, it should be noted that in his initial analysis of the passions of the soul, Aquinas identifies only one, out of eleven, that we would describe as a moral passion (*ST* I-II q. 23, a. 4). In what follows, I refer to the moral passions in the plural, and in this way, I go beyond what Aquinas explicitly says. I cannot argue the point here, but I cannot see any reason in principle why Aquinas's list of the passions could not be expanded to include primary moral passions in addition to anger, and I assume as much in what follows.

Passions and Dispositions: The Remote Principles of Morality

Let me begin by laying out the general parameters of our inquiry. Aquinas, following Aristotle, says that all living creatures operate through processes of responsive and active engagement with their environments, in accordance with the species-specific, dynamic principles of activity comprising the soul. In the higher animals, including ourselves, these processes are mediated through the animal's perceptions of its environment, and driven, as it were, by desires and aversions, or more complex affective responses, emerging out of those perceptions (*In de anima* III.6, paras. 655-670; *ST* I q. 80, a. 1; q. 83, a. 1; I-II q. 6, a. 2). Aquinas refers to these desires in general terms as inclinations, adding that the proper act of an appetite is an inclination of this kind (*ST* I-II q. 50, a.5, *ad.* 1). Thus, appetites are capacities through which a living creature is capable of desiring or detesting some perceived object, and moving itself to act accordingly. As such, they play a central role in the overall operations of a sentient animal. Once elicited, an inclination initiates some kind of self-motion within the creature, through which it pursues, avoids, or resists some perceived desirable, noxious, or threatening object (*ST* I q. 81, a. 1; I-II q. 22, a. 2). More specifically, the passions are appetites of a distinctive kind, capacities to respond affectively to objects perceived through the senses, including remembered or imagined representations of perceived objects. Because these inclinations stem from sense perceptions, they presuppose bodily change of some kind, if only through the functioning of the sense organs, and they are naturally targeted towards particular objects of desire and aversion (*ST* I-II q. 22, aa. 1, 3).[6]

[6] Or more specifically, the inclinations of the passions correspond to particular kinds of objects, but not always to specific objects, directly perceived in the environment. The point is that the passions are oriented to specific kinds of desirable or undesirable objects, or relations, or states of affairs, grasped immediately through the senses or represented through memory and imagination, rather than to the desirable or undesirable, identified as such through some general description. For example, one might

In nonhuman animals, the passions operate spontaneously in such a way as to move the animal to act effectively in relation to its environment.[7] Through the operations of what Aquinas identifies as an estimative sense, the nonhuman animal perceives its environment in terms set by its own natural needs and vulnerabilities, and responds and acts accordingly (*ST* I q. 78, a. 4; q. 81, a. 3). In this way, the animal is moved to operations which promote its life, well-being, reproductive functions, and the like (*ST* I q. 81, a. 3). The animal's engagement with its environment is thus determined by its overall desires and aversions, in such a way that it perceives the world in terms of what is good or bad for an animal of its kind. At the same time, it is important to realize that these perceptions and desires will normally reflect an accurate grasp of the world as it is—otherwise, the animal would not be long for this world. Generally, the objects that the animal perceives as suitable for food, an appropriate mate, potential danger, and the like, really are such, seen in reference to the kind of animal that is in question; the animal's perceptions are narrowly focused, but sound and adequate for its purposes, normally so at any rate.

Like the other higher animals, human beings are tethered to their immediate environment through sensory perceptions, leading to spontaneous inclinations of desire or aversion grounded in the sensual appetites, that is to say, the passions. Because they are grounded in sensory perceptions, including imagined or remembered as well as immediate images, these kinds of inclinations presuppose some kind of bodily change, and they are directed towards particular objects. In both respects, human passions are essentially similar to their counterparts in nonhuman animals, and Aquinas accordingly identifies the inclinations of the passions as actions of a kind that we share with the other animals (*ST* I-II q. 6 intro.). At the same time, there is at least one critical difference between human passions and their counterparts among nonhuman animals.

Rational creatures, like other animals, experience spontaneous sensual perceptions, desires, and aversions, which elicit corresponding actions of pursuit, avoidance, and the like. But in us, these perceptions and feelings are not innately tied to determinate kinds of objects in the way that the passions of nonhuman animals are. This indeterminacy is by no means a defect in itself—rather, it gives our perceptions and feelings a kind of plasticity, which enables them to be shaped by rational formation and reflection (*ST* I q, 81, a. 3). The squirrels in our

---

have a passionate desire for a steak, which need not be identified with this or that steak, in contrast to desiring something suitable for nutrition, which might or might not be a steak. The latter would be an inclination of the will, presupposing some rational judgment. For a helpful discussion of this distinction, see Robert Miner, *Thomas Aquinas on the Passions: A Study of Summa Theologiae Ia2ae 22-48* (Cambridge: Cambridge University Press, 2009), 19-25

[7] For further details, see *Thomas Aquinas on the Passions*, 69-76.

backyard naturally perceive our garden as a kind of a salad bar, and from their perspective they are entirely justified in doing so. But by the same token, they cannot see these bulbs and plants in any other way, as an ensemble of living creatures in its own right, or a lovely pattern of colors and scents, or the remote cause of a particular danger, represented by my exasperated husband. In contrast, even the sensory perceptions of a rational creature presuppose some degree of rational formation, and by the same token, we can learn to perceive in more than one way, to shape our perceptions in one direction rather than another, and the like.[8]

The indeterminacy of human passions is the immediate consequence of the indeterminacy of perception. In themselves, our passions are capacities for characteristic kinds of affective responses—for example, the passion of love is a capacity to desire what is pleasing to the senses (*ST* I-II q. 26, a. 1).[9] But for the human animal, unlike nonhumans, this general capacity is not correlated to any particular object, or even any generic kind of object. We must be taught to see the world rightly, both in relation to our own desires and limitations, and from other perspectives as well, including both intersubjective perspectives and those which are more or less detached from what we might call a human point of view. In the process, we will also, inevitably, be taught how to feel, what to desire and what to reject or flee. Our perceptual capacities and our passions will necessarily be formed together, because the passions are naturally correlated with certain kinds of perceptions. Once we learn that something is potentially edible, we will be disposed to respond to it with hunger and delight, thus bringing it within the broad field of possible objects of love. Because we are tethered to our world through sensory perceptions and desires, each implies the other in complex but intelligible ways, and they must be shaped together in order to function at all.

This, in my view, explains why Aquinas says that the passions of the human person must be shaped by habits, that is to say, stable dispositions orienting these appetites towards determinate kinds of objects.[10] Prior to formation, the passions can yield nothing more than unfocused desires and aversions, which cannot elicit action, precisely because they lack a determinate object towards which (or away from

---

[8] Again, Miner provides a very helpful discussion of this point; see *Thomas Aquinas on the Passions*, 76-82.

[9] This observation is complicated by the fact that Aquinas discusses both sensual and rational love in the first question devoted to specific passions, that is, *ST* I-II q. 26. As he goes on to explain, love as a passion, properly so called, is a capacity of the concupiscable part of the soul, which is the origin of simple inclinations of desire and aversion (*ST* I-II q. 26, aa. 1, 2).

[10] I develop this argument in more detail in "Why Are the Habits Necessary? An Inquiry into Aquinas's Moral Psychology" *Oxford Studies in Medieval Philosophy* Vol. 1 (2013), 113-35.

which) the individual might direct her operations. These capacities for responsive feeling need to be formed through ongoing processes of training and education, so that they will be elicited and expressed in appropriate ways, in accordance with perceived and imagined desirable and noxious objects. This presupposes an extended process of formation, initially under the guidance of caretakers and then through the individual's own experience and reflection, guided throughout by general reasoned considerations. (These need not be good reasons, by the way—these processes of formation can lead to either good or bad dispositions, virtues or vices.) At the same time, it is important to realize that while human passions must be shaped in accordance with rational judgments of some kind in order to function, they continue to play an indispensable role in the overall operations of the human animal. Reason shapes the passions, on Aquinas's account, but does not replace them; the passions retain a kind of independence, insofar as they can elicit inclinations prior to and even contrary to one's rational judgments (*ST* I-II q. 56, a. 4).

This brings us to an important point. Aquinas would agree with de Waal that it is a mistake to think of human morality as something added onto an immoral core. He would question the adjective "immoral" in this context, since neither nonhuman animals nor pre-rational children are capable of either moral or immoral choices. Nonetheless, he would agree that there is something odd about the image of a moral capacity that is grafted onto a core of essentially non-rational perceptions and feelings. However, for Aquinas this image misses the mark because for a rational creature, there is no aspect of conscious functioning, including sensory perceptions and desires, which is not qualified in some way by rational judgments and the desires that these elicit. A mature, functionally normal human being perceives, feels, and acts in accordance with a conceptual framework of some kind and ongoing processes of rational deliberation, judgments and choices, without which he could not function properly at all, even at the most basic levels of perception and sensory desires. At the same time, the diverse qualities that go to make up the agent's rationality can only function effectively if they are integrated into his conscious functioning at this basic level. Rational thought always depends on the starting points generated by perceptions, and the agent's will and his powers of deliberation and choice would not be effectively engaged unless he were tethered to his environment through an ongoing dynamism of perceptions and desires.

Thus, de Waal is right to say that without emotions, or the operations of the passions, the agent would not be moved to act at all, and furthermore, the passions can operate in such a way as to elicit judgments and responses without the mediating force of deliberation. But that does not mean that these operate apart from, or prior to reason—they have been shaped by rational considerations, and these help to shape, and are in turn expressed through, our gut feelings and immediate intuitions. These rational considerations cannot be elicited from sensory perceptions alone—they require, in addition, rational principles which Aquinas regards as foundational for moral reasoning.

MORAL PASSIONS AND PRINCIPLES OF OBLIGATION

The first point that needs to be made, in order to extend Aquinas's general analysis of the passions to moral passions, is simply that the latter are passions—that is to say, they fit the same general template that applies to the passions generally. They operate through inclinations elicited by sensory perceptions of some kind, and they are directed towards a particular object. This may not be immediately apparent, because the inclinations of the moral passions are generally more complex than straightforward desires and aversions, and they do not seem to be tethered in the same way to specific perceptions or imagined or remembered images. This worry can be set aside, however, because Aquinas construes the object of a capacity in such a way as to include the kind of operation that it characteristically elicits, as well as the entity or state of affairs constituting the aim of the operation (*ST* I q. 77, a. 3). In particular, following on Aristotle he analyzes the passion of anger in terms of a perception of undeserved injury, calling forth a desire to avenge oneself by inflicting pain on the offender (*ST* I-II q. 46, a. 4). The passion of anger and its corresponding inclination would thus fit the general template of the moral passions and emotions as we understand them. In the first place, it appears to presuppose a kind of moral sense, more specifically, a sense of justice (*ST* I-II q. 46, a. 7), and secondly, it is relational, that is to say, it is aimed at a kind of action which brings the agent into some kind of relation with another.

On a first reading, Aquinas's analysis of anger might be taken to imply that the similarities between the seeming moral emotions of the animals and distinctively human moral passions and emotions are superficial at best. In the course of considering whether the passion of anger is accompanied with reason, he considers the objection that brute animals, who lack reason, also exhibit anger. In response, he reminds us that brute animals have a natural instinct conferred on them by divine reason, through which they operate in ways that resemble rational judgments, desires and actions (*ST* I-II q. 46, a. 4 *ad.* 2). Taken by itself, this remark might suggest that nonhuman animals follow reasonable principles mechanically, operating in accordance with divine guidance. This would hardly be a helpful perspective from which to make sense of the continuities between the moral emotions of nonhuman and human animals.

Yet this line of interpretation does not take account of Aquinas's overall analysis of the role of the passions in nonhuman and human animals. As we have seen, he claims that nonhuman animals are moved to act through conscious apprehension of desirable and undesirable objects, eliciting inclinations of pursuit, avoidance, and the like. These processes are grounded in God's creative wisdom, but they also stem from the creature's own intrinsic principles of operation. When we return to Aquinas's remarks on anger, we see that he develops the comparison between nonhuman and human anger in such a way as to bring out the continuities implied by his overall account of the passions as intrinsic principles of operation.

Having established that there is a connection between anger and rationality, he goes on to ask whether anger presupposes some kind of relation of justice, which implies that we can only be angry with other rational creatures (*ST* I-II q. 46, a. 7). He replies that this is true with respect to anger properly so called, since the passion of anger presupposes a sense of undue injury, and aims at vindication, which is, or can be, an act of justice. Yet he is well aware that we do sometimes get angry with irrational objects, like a leaky pen or an unruly horse. In response, he once again draws a comparison between nonhuman and human animals. Once again, he reminds us that through natural instinct, nonhuman animals act as if they had the use of reason. But now he goes on to explain that this instinct operates through the animal's imagination, that is to say, its capacity to form *phantasia* or images drawn from its sensory perceptions (*ST* I-II q. 46, a. 7 *ad.* 1; cf. I q. 78, a. 4). Thus, the anger exhibited by nonhuman animals is not simply an unconscious or mechanical response. It functions in the same way as the other passions exhibited by these animals, through affective inclinations elicited by consciously held images of one's environment. What is more, Aquinas continues, we too have imagination, in addition to reason, and we are therefore capable of the same kind of anger that we find in the other animals, triggered through a perception or image of being harmed, and expressed through an immediate impulse to lash out. This is not the kind of anger that is distinctive to us as human beings, but we are capable of it, nonetheless.

In spite of the initial impression generated by his remarks at *ST* I-II q. 46, a. 4, Aquinas's treatment of anger in nonhuman and human animals is consistent with his overall account of the passions. In nonhuman animals, and sometimes in humans, the inclinations of the passions emerge in response to perceptions or images, which are in some way affectively charged. It is true that in the case of anger and other moral passions, these images are not tied to specific objects in the animal's environment in the same way as most desires and aversions are. A bonobo perceives a nice orange as a snack and takes it, while she perceives a tiger as a threat and runs from it. But when she perceives one of her fellows in evident distress, and responds with apparent sorrow and a desire to give comfort, what is it that she perceives? It seems too quick to say that she simply perceives another bonobo, or even that she perceives one of her fellows as sorrowing. Neither description captures what it is about this perception that elicits the complex passion, distress at another's sorrow combined with a desire to comfort. If the bonobo were simply saddened by the perception of another's suffering, perhaps through a kind of emotional contagion, we would expect a response of avoidance or flight. What moves her to offer comfort instead?

The moral emotions are so called because they prompt an animal to enter into some kind of relation to another. This presupposes a perception of the other in terms of its relation to the creature, that is to say, as an appropriate target for some kind of activity. The kindly bonobo does not just perceive her sorrowing fellow as an object in her environment; she sees him as eliciting her comfort in some way. Thus, she perceives him in the terms set by her natural inclinations towards activities of certain kinds—just as she perceives an orange as the target of her activities of grasping and eating. So far, we do not need to qualify Aquinas's overall account of the passions in order to account for the moral emotion of compassion as the inclination of a complex passion prompting both sorrow and active engagement. We can account for the bonobo's behavior without assuming anything other than a straightforward apprehension of a particular object, mediated through perceptions and images informed by an estimative sense. In this case, the object in question is not a physical entity, but an entity of a certain kind, a fellow creature, seen as related to her in a certain way, as appropriately to be comforted.

At this point, let me try to forestall misunderstanding. I am not saying that the nonhuman animal necessarily perceives its fellows as such—that is to say, as independent entities, similar to and yet distinct from the creature itself. Possibly, it does, but these kinds of perceptions are not necessary to the processes we are examining. Nor do we need to assume that the animal brings to mind, as it were, any considerations of the other's situation, any sense of how it would feel in the other's place, the appropriateness of responding in one way rather than another, or the like. My point is rather that a nonhuman animal does not need to reflect in these terms at all in order to relate to its fellows in appropriate ways. Its perceptions of others in its immediate social circle would seem to be perceptions of relations, mediated through images that bring together certain patterns of behavior on the part of another with one's responses. These relations, and the responsive operations that they elicit, are as much a part of the animal's immediate environment and its dynamic interactions with that environment as the ongoing array of edibles and threats, eliciting desire and consumption, or fear and avoidance. The animal does not need to think about its fellows as such in order to respond appropriately to them, any more than it needs to think of an orange as fruit, in order to eat it.

This example brings us to the second issue flagged above. The inclinations of a nonhuman animal to eat a nice piece of fruit or to flee a predator fit within the overall form of life appropriate to the animal, because generally, fruit is edible and predators are dangerous. The animal's perceptions are narrowly focused on its needs and desires, but within these limits they are generally trustworthy. But can we say the same thing about its perceptions of the appropriate relations between itself and its fellows? We can best address this question by starting with the inclinations and operations in question, rather than the perceptions eliciting them. What are the moral passions and their corresponding inclinations and behaviors good for—that is to say, what place do they have in the overall operations and the form of life proper to living creatures of a certain kind? Clearly, consuming food and avoiding predators promote the survival of the individual, and mating promotes the ongoing existence of the species. But how do social behaviors fit into the overall form of life proper to a given kind of animal?

Once we have posed the question in these terms, it almost answers itself. That is, social animals are characterized by a social form of life, in which populations are held together through pattered interactions, which both sustain the individual throughout its life course and promote the ongoing existence of the group.[11] Life within a community, held together through dynamic, structured relations, is natural to certain kinds of animals, and they cannot flourish, individually or collectively, apart from these patterned interactions. By relating to one another in given ways, individuals sustain these patterned interactions, by participating in core relations of dominance, submission, and cooperation, reinforcing good behavior and cohesion through rewards, consoling behaviors, and the like, and discouraging disruptive behavior through retaliation, withholding, or non- cooperation. Correlatively, when an animal perceives the other in terms of its relation to that other, its perception is grounded in the objective normative demands of a kind of social existence. This perception, in turn, elicits an inclination towards some kind of activity, which will normally fit with the way of life proper to this kind of creature, and which will as such serve to promote the overall functioning of the group.

So far, the moral passions would seem to fit within the parameters of Aquinas's general analysis of the passions. They are relatively complex passions, but they nonetheless can be analyzed in terms of desires elicited by certain kinds of sensory perceptions and images, moving the animal to act in appropriate ways. Nonhuman animals do not need to reflect on these perceptions or deliberate about them, because they are naturally disposed to perceive others of their circle in terms of their appropriate relations to others, and to act accordingly. By the same

[11] On this point, see *Moral Origins*, 89-131.

token, the moral emotions of nonhuman animals need not be mediated through general conceptions of altruism, respect, or obligation. A bonobo does not need to have a general grasp of what it means to be a bonobo just like me, or what it means to be obliged to offer comfort to another, in order to respond appropriately to her suffering mate, here and now. She spontaneously perceives the other as to be comforted, and acts accordingly.

A Thomistic approach to the moral emotions as passions can thus account for both the similarities between human and nonhuman animals, and the differences that remain. We too are social animals, naturally suited to a way of life sustained through patterns of relationships with others. Like other kinds of social animals, we are initially drawn into these relations through the inclinations of the moral passions, which are initially elicited through perceptions or images of others calling forth spontaneous responses of aid, comfort, withdrawal, punishment, and the like. The moral passions of young children would presumably function in this way, and as Aquinas observes with respect to anger, mature, rational men and women remain capable of these kinds of spontaneous responses to others. At the same time, immature passions of these kinds are limited and ineffectual without processes of formation, leading to the development of stable dispositions to respond in certain ways and to avoid others. This point calls for some further attention, however, because the moral emotions in us are not exactly parallel to simple desires and aversions for particular objects, and call for a somewhat different kind of formation.

As we recall, the desires and aversions of a rational creature are innately relatively indeterminate, just as her perceptions are. We need to be taught how to perceive and how to feel, through processes of formation leading to stable dispositions of the passions. To some extent, the moral emotions are similarly indeterminate, but less so than simple desires and aversions. The moral emotions appear to be structured in such a way as to reflect some aspect of the perceived relations that elicit them, even prior to processes of training and formation. We recall that Aquinas says that in its fully human form, anger depends on a kind of reasoning, incorporating as it does a judgment that some perceived slight or imbalance is not to be borne. If our moral emotions already encode this much, why do they need any kind of formation at all?

In us, the moral passions are in themselves relatively determinate, at least seen in contrast to other innate desires and aversions. Nonetheless, we cannot effectively act on these emotions until they have been shaped and integrated through the formation of stable dispositions, inclining us to respond to others in characteristic ways. While the moral passions are more structured than most passions, they are still too indeterminate to lead to appropriate kinds of actions, which reflect the overall human good in the relevant ways. What is more, we simply have too many of them, including contradictory inclinations towards the same person at the same time. Again, this problem does not arise for nonhumans, because for them, the moral emotions spontaneously reflect the patterns of relationship appropriate to the group in question. But human perceptions of relations cannot function in this same way for us, in key part because we perceive and relate to other men and women in more than one way, eliciting diverse and sometimes contrary inclinations. King David was angry with Absalom, considered as a rebel against his throne, and he wanted to kill him—yet he also loved him desperately as his son, and wanted to protect him. He could not act on both inclinations at once, and he stood in need of some overarching disposition which would have allowed him to perceive and to respond to this individual appropriately, all things considered.

This brings us to a key point. The moral passions, our capacities for moral emotions, stand in need of some kind of formation, in order to be amenable to integration and coordination. Yet so long as we stay at the level of the passions and the moral emotions springing from them, we cannot account for their formation as a kind of ensemble of responses. In themselves, and presupposing proper functioning, the inclinations of the moral passions do depend on a real aspect of our environment, namely, the responsiveness appropriate to this particular situation, here and now. But in themselves, they cannot provide a basis for coordination, because they do not represent the kinds of general considerations that would enable us to place a range of responses in an overall context, and to shape them accordingly. In order to do so, it is necessary to move to another level of perception and desire, which will allow us some purchase on the diverse kinds of other-related norms that inform the moral emotions themselves. We need, in other words, to introduce general principles of other-regard and obligation, which will provide a framework for integrating, and where necessary, correcting our diverse responses to others.

Once again, it is helpful to compare nonhuman and human responses of the relevant kind. Nonhumans do not appear to make use of general normative categories in their interactions with others, and we can readily see why not. They spontaneously perceive how they stand in relation to others, in accordance with internalized patterns of relationship sustaining the social unit in which they share. Men and women, in contrast, do not spontaneously perceive their fellows in terms of a pattern of interrelationships sustaining a collective way of life. We as individuals can perceive one another in more than one way, each of which elicits a different range of emotional responses and behavioral interactions. What is more, human societies do not spontaneously organize themselves into a determinate pattern of life, in accordance with a fixed, species-specific way of life. Human societies must take account of the basic facts of our animal and social life, of course, but there are indefinitely many ways of doing so, which remain indeterminate prior to collective determinations concerning the proper forms of marriage and kinship, ownership and exchange, authority and power, and much more. This relative priority of rational determinations is a logical, rather than a temporal priority, but it implies that the structuring systems of any given human society will be to some degree contingent. For this reason, too, children cannot simply grow into a way of life, spontaneously grasped through perceptions of others in relation to the self—they must be taught, in general and categorical terms, to understand their communal way of life and to identify their place in the web of relations that it implies.

Where do these general principles come from? Given the overall terms of Aquinas's analysis of the passions, they cannot stem from the moral passions taken by themselves, because these inclinations of desire, aversion, and responsiveness are intrinsically directed to particular persons and situations—just as all passions are. Certainly, the moral emotions represent responses to veridical perceptions of the agent's place in a system of relations, which normally, if not infallibly, reflect genuine aspects of a network of interrelationships. Thus, they provide the starting points for rational reflection, as well as eliciting it. Nonetheless, in order to reflect effectively on these diverse and partial perceptions, men and women need to draw on general principles, which can only emerge out of our capacities for abstract and categorical thought.[12]

This may sound a bit chilly, but nothing in Aquinas's account implies that our interactions with others should be, or can be conducted on a basis of reasoned forbearance alone. Although he does not develop this point at length, Aquinas comments more than once on the interrelationships between perception and reason, passion and will in practical reason and action. He observes that just as the intellect can only grasp general concepts as these are mediated through particulars, so the will can only be moved through the mediation of particular objects of desire (*ST* I q. 80, a. 2 *ad.* 2). What is more, just as speculative reason can only operate in and through the grasp of general forms in particulars, so the general principles of practical reason would be empty and ineffectual, without the specification drawn from particular images of the desirable and the undesirable (*In de Anima* III. 16, paras. 845-46). By implication, general principles of other-regarding morality would be empty, apart from the perceptions of right and wrong relations that correspond to the moral passions. Although he would insist on the necessary role of rational judgments and desires in human

---

[12] Aquinas believes that the first principles of other regarding morality, together with basic concepts of transgressive harm and obligation, are innate – see *ST* II-II q. 79, a. 1.

morality, Aquinas also appears to believe that our reason and will cannot function apart from our spontaneous perceptions of particular situations and the emotions that these elicit, and in this respect he is closer to de Waal than we might initially have expected.

For Aquinas, the passions and the will work together to move the human agent to act and to enable him to do so in a coherent and salutary way. They can function in this way because each is responsive to the agent's reality, through partial but necessary perceptions and images, or through general principles and the abstract concepts and norms that these yield. These observations are generally true, but they are especially relevant to our understanding of the moral emotions. Seen in terms of Aquinas's overall schema, these emotions are grounded in an apprehension of one's place in a social world, and elicit spontaneous responses and actions oriented towards maintaining that place. These perceptions are partial and incomplete, and the moral emotions they generate are not sufficient as guides to correct action in a complex human world. That is why they stand in need of integration and formation through practical reason and will, in order to operate in an appropriate way. At the same time, the moral emotions represent our most immediate and direct engagement with our immediate social world and the men and women we encounter there. They tether us to the particularities of our situation, apart from which our general principles would have no meaning. As such, they are indispensable to human life—not sufficient in themselves, but necessary nonetheless. Integrated into an overall commitment to relate rightly to others, within the context of an overall sense of one's place in a web of relations, they elicit immediate responses to the needs of others, and direct our attention to their due claims. As de Waal would remind us, we cannot grasp the immediate practical implications of our commitments, or carry through on the best inclinations of a good will, unless these capacities for responsiveness are in place.[13] M

[13] An earlier version of this article was delivered as a lecture under the title of "Judgements of Desire: A Thomistic Perspective on the Moral Emotions in Nonhuman and Human Animals," at the Ian Ramsey Center, Trinity College, Oxford, March 7, 2013, and I am grateful to those present for many helpful questions and comments. I would also like to express my gratitude to two anonymous readers for *The Journal of Moral Theology* for many helpful comments and suggestions. Any remaining mistakes are of course my own.

Journal of Moral Theology, Vol. 3, No. 2 (2014): 109-129

Speaking Theologically of Animal Rights

James E. Helmer

THE ISSUES OF THE WELFARE AND RIGHTS of non-human animals have gained prominence in philosophical ethics over the past thirty years, owing largely though not exclusively to the work of Peter Singer and Tom Regan.[1] In spite of this extensive philosophical engagement, however, until recently these issues have received comparatively limited attention by ethicists working within the Christian theological tradition (and within Roman Catholic moral theology more specifically), which has for the most part remained decidedly anthropocentric in its orientation.[2] Fortunately, in spite of the dominance of anthropocentrism and of speciesism within the theological tradition, there has been an increasing shift in recent Christian theology towards a deeper consideration of the theological and ethical significance of non-human animal species—and most specifically, of the cognitive and affective capacities of non-human animals, and of why non-human animals might be considered appropriate subjects of justice and moral rights.

Long before this recent turn, the pioneering work of Anglican theologian Andrew Linzey introduced the issue of the ethical significance of non-human animals into contemporary theological discussion, with

---

[1] Peter Singer, *Animal Liberation*, Reissue Edition (San Francisco: Harper, 2009); Tom Regan, *The Case for Animal Rights* (Berkeley: University of California Press, 1983, 2004).

[2] On anthropocentrism in the Christian theological tradition, see David Clough, *On Animals,* Volume One: *Systematic Theology* (New York: Continuum, 2012); Charles Camosy, *For Love of Animals: Christian Ethics, Consistent Action* (Cincinnati: Franciscan, 2013) and "Other Animals as Persons? A Roman Catholic Inquiry," in *Animals as Religious Subjects: Transdisciplinary Perspectives*, ed. Celia Deane-Drummond, Rebecca Artinian-Kaiser, and David Clough (New York: Continuum, 2013), 259-78. In suggesting that the Christian theological tradition has been predominantly anthropocentric, one must acknowledge the emergence of various eco-theological perspectives which are more biocentric and which mirror theologically various contemporary philosophical perspectives (e.g., deep ecology, ecofeminism). However, these perspectives differ in important ways from those working in the area of animal ethics and animal theology, as various proponents have argued. On this point in addition to Clough, *On Animals*, see Celia Deane-Drummond, *Eco-Theology* (London: Darton, Longman and Todd, 2008); Andrew Linzey, *Animal Theology* (London: SCM Press, 1994) and *Creatures of the Same God: Explorations in Animal Theology* (Brooklyn: Lantern, 2007, 2009).

his (now classic) *Christianity and the Rights of Animals*.[3] In conversation with both philosophical and theological sources, Linzey's work has been formative for many of those who are considering the issue of animal ethics from a Christian theological perspective, and it has prompted significant theological engagement with fundamental and critical questions in relation to the moral standing and treatment of non-human animals: Why do non-human animals matter and why should we care about them? What is their moral status? Is there anything distinctive (or unique) about animals in general that is morally significant? Are non-human animals persons? Even if non-human animals are not persons, do they still matter ethically? Do they possess either inviolable dignity or inherent moral worth or intrinsic moral value? Can non-human animals be bearers of rights? And perhaps most importantly: Can a theological perspective provide distinctive insights in considering these questions?

In a recent review essay of Linzey's work, British theologian David Grummett has suggested that while Linzey and others have given considerable attention to the issue of the moral status of animals as "moral patients"—or objects of moral concern—there needs to significantly more constructive theological engagement with the question of the moral agency of animals, particularly as this relates to the issue of animal rights.[4] Grummett's suggestion is an especially fitting one for two reasons. First, the general discussion of issues of moral agency has featured centrally in recent philosophical attempts to formulate a defensible theory of animal rights. Second, focused consideration has been given to the issue of whether the possession and exercise of capacities typically associated with moral agency is a necessary condition for assigning moral standing to human beings and to non-human animals.[5]

---

[3] Andrew Linzey, *Christianity and the Rights of Animals* (New York: Crossroad, 1987).

[4] David Grummett, "Animals in Christian Theology," *Religion Compass* Vol. 5, no. 10 (2011), 579-88.

[5] See for example, David DeGrazia, *Taking Animals Seriously: Mental Life and Moral Status* (Cambridge: Cambridge University Press, 1996); Mark Rowlands, *Animal Rights: Moral Theory and Practice* (New York: Palgrave Macmillan, 2003), *Animals Like Us* (New York: Verso, 2002), and *Can Animals be Moral?* (New York: Oxford University Press, 2012); Gary Steiner, *Animals and the Moral Community: Mental Life, Moral Status, and Kinship* (New York: Columbia University Press, 2008); and Marian Stamp Dawkins, *Why Animals Matter: Animal Consciousness, Animal Welfare, and Human Well-Being* (New York: Oxford University Press, 2012). These are examples of analytic philosophers, but work is also being done in the continental tradition of philosophy. See, for example, Cary Wolfe, *Animal Rites: American Culture, The Discourse of Species and Posthumanist Theory* (Chicago: University of Chicago Press, 2003) and *Before the Law: Humans and Other Animals in Biopolitical Frame* (Chicago: University of Chicago Press, 2012).

In this essay, I engage with the issue of the (alleged) normative relationship between moral agency and moral rights, and more specifically, with the claim that the possession and exercise of various capacities that are typically associated with moral agency are a necessary condition for ascribing moral rights either to human beings or to non-human animals. Working by way of analogy from the case of rights ascription in the case of human beings, I shall argue for the conceptual coherence of ascribing rights to (at least some) non-human animals on the basis of their status both as moral patients and as moral subjects.[6] While the category of moral patiency, like that of moral agency, is one

---

[6] My claim, here, is deliberately open-ended for more than a few reasons.

I am concerned with establishing the conceptual coherence of extending by way of analogy the concept of moral rights to the non-human animal context. The two conceptual bridges that I am employing to do so are those concepts of moral patients and moral subjects. In the animal rights literature, the concept of "moral patient" is frequently contrasted with and variously developed in contradistinction to that of "moral agent." The locus classicus of the distinction is to be found in the animal rights theory developed by Tom Regan, where Regan argues for the ascription of a basic right to respect based on considerations of moral patiency. Regan characterizes moral patients more narrowly as "subjects of a life" who fail to qualify as moral agents, but who are nevertheless "morally considerable" or possess moral standing (in Regan's account, their possession of intrinsic value and their capacity for experiential well-being). However, others (e.g., Rowlands, 2012) have employed a broader conception of the moral patient than that employed by Regan, and in this essay, I adopt this broader usage. In general, to be a moral patient is to possess moral status or standing, to be morally considerable and an object of moral respect and concern, and thus, to be the beneficiary of various duties and obligations on the part of moral agents. For various proposals concerning the distinction between moral agency and moral patiency, see Regan, *The Case for Animal Rights*; Mary Anne Warren, *Moral Status: Obligations to Persons and Other Living Things* (New York: Oxford University Press, 1997); Gary Francione, *Animals, Property and the Law* (Philadelphia: Temple University Press, 1995), *Rain without Thunder: The Ideology of the Animal Rights Movement* (Philadelphia: Temple University Press, 1996), and *Animals as Persons: Essays on the Abolition of Animal Exploitation* (New York: Columbia University Press, 2008); and Rowlands, *Animal Rights: Moral Theory and Practice* and *Can Animals be Moral?*.

The grounds for rights ascription can be plural, as can the content of the particular rights that are ascribed to particular beings. A non-human animal (e.g., a dog) may by analogy possess some of the various rights that a human being possesses (e.g., the right not to be tortured) but may not possess others. The rights in question will be to some extent determined by the nature, interests, and well-being of the being in question. We can not only articulate different criterial properties (e.g., dignity, personhood, intrinsic value, sentience, interests, agency) as the basis for moral considerability and the ascription of rights, but as we shall see, these criteria themselves may admit of degrees, which may (though not need) translate into a sliding scale. For further discussion of these issues, see Warren, *Moral Status* and also DeGrazia, *Taking Animals Seriously*, "Equal Consideration and Unequal Moral Status," *Southern Journal of Philosophy* Vol. 31, no. 1 (Spring 1993), 17-31 and "Moral Status as a Matter of Degree?" *Southern Journal of Philosophy* Vol. 46, no. 2 (Summer 2008), 181-98; and Alasdair Cochrane, *Animal Rights without Liberation: Applied Ethics and Human Obligations* (New York: Columbia University Press, 2012).

that has been well-exercised in philosophical discussions of animal rights, the category of moral subjectivity—in the sense in which I am employing the term—is a bridge concept encompassing aspects of moral patiency and moral agency that has until recently received significantly less attention. This lacuna is regrettable given that the concept of moral subjectivity can serve to advance the existing philosophical and theological discussion of animal rights in order to better unfold our normative commitments. Throughout this essay, the position that I shall be challenging is one which exclusively associates the assignment of moral standing, and in turn moral rights, with capacities associated with the exercise of moral agency.

The essay proceeds as follows. The next part of the article provides a relatively brief discussion of the paradigmatic case of rights attribution, which is the case of moral rights attributed to human beings. In what follows, I make no attempt to engage the Catholic moral tradition comprehensively, but simply to sketch out in skeletal outline the key elements of a contemporary Catholic perspective on moral rights in relation to human beings, and to draw on the contemporary perspective of Catholic social thought in doing so. Given the substantial breadth of recent ecclesial statements expressing rights discourse, I attend to two primary sources: the *Compendium of the Social Doctrine of the Church* and the 2004 International Theological Commission Document, "Communion and Stewardship: Human Persons Created in the Image of God."[7] My rationale for beginning with the paradigmatic case of human beings will be fairly obvious, as it enables us to identify the reasons that we consider human beings to be morally considerable and to be the appropriate bearers of moral rights. In contrast, the rationale for beginning with a thick theological perspective may be far less obvious, given that rights discourse is often intended to function as a kind of "lingua franca," transcending the particularity of religious traditions, and thus as serviceable to public discourse in culturally and religiously plural societies. If rights discourse is indeed to

[7] Pontifical Council for Justice and Peace, "Compendium of the Social Doctrine of the Church, www.vatican.va/roman_curia/pontifical_councils/justpeace/documents/-rc_pc_justpeace_doc_20060526_compendio-dott-soc_en.html. International Theological Commission, "Communion and Stewardship: Human Persons Created in the Image of God" www.vatican.va/roman_curia/congregations/cfaith/cti_documents/-rc_con_cfaith_doc_20040723_communion-stewardship_en.html.

Given the breadth and richness of the tradition of Catholic social thought, to limit consideration of the tradition's views to only two ecclesial documents will no doubt appear unduly restrictive or even arbitrary. These two documents have been selected because they provide a concise and fairly recent encapsulation of the tradition's views concerning these issues, and other documents might serve equally well (e.g., John XXIII's *Pacem in Terris* or John Paul II's *Redemptor Hominis* on human rights; recent statements in the area of bioethics, such as *Dignitas Personae*, as expressions of the tradition's moral personalism).

play a "bridge-building" role analogous to that of natural law discourse, then how can a specifically theological perspective on the rights of non-human animals contribute to a general public consideration of the issue of animal welfare? While this question expresses a legitimate concern, it should not dominate the present discussion, which is addressed primarily to those thinking within the intellectual horizons of the Catholic tradition and is intended to persuade those who situate themselves within Catholic Christianity that a re-consideration of the idea of the rights of non-human animals is theologically and ethically warranted.[8]

Following this sketch of the moral foundations of human rights, I then consider the issue of the analogous extension of moral rights to non-human animals, and argue that although the tradition initially appears to preclude this possibility, that the extension is consonant with the logic of moral rights employed by the tradition in the paradigmatic case of human beings. What makes this analogous extension possible, I suggest, is, first, that as creatures expressing the goodness of divine creation, non-human animals are bearers of inherent or intrinsic value—and thus worthy of moral respect—and second, that as bearers of essential moral interests and as creatures who flourish (or to fail to flourish), non-human animals can be properly regarded as bearers of moral rights—and thus entitled to moral concern. In making these arguments, I focus on the issue of ascribing rights to non-human animals on the basis of their status as moral patients. In the final section of the essay, I consider the issue of ascribing rights to non-human animals on the basis of their status as moral subjects.

Moral Personality: The Basis for Ascribing Moral Rights

As I have already indicated, I will make no attempt to discuss or to elaborate the richness and diversity of contemporary Roman Catholic perspectives concerning the moral foundations of human rights, but only to provide a skeletal outline of the Catholic social tradition's perspective by engaging with two recent texts: the *Compendium of the Social Doctrine of the Church* (2006) (hereafter, *Compendium*) and

---

[8] Two points by way of an additional preliminary methodological note: First, the argument of the essay is directed towards those who accept the vision of the human person and moral rights variously expressed in the tradition of Catholic social teaching. In this essay the expression "the tradition" functions primarily as shorthand for the magisterial documents of Catholic social teaching, but not in such a way as to preclude broader theological reflection. Second, although the discussion that follows is not robustly biblical (in the sense of elucidating theological doctrines), it is nevertheless theological in the sense that it proceeds within a theological framework and is concerned to exhibit theological integrity (rather than distinctiveness). For more on the idea of theological integrity, see *Nigel Biggar, Behaving in Public: How to Do Christian Ethics* (Grand Rapids: Eerdmans, 2011).

the International Theological Commission Document, "Communion and Stewardship: Human Persons Created in the Image of God" (2004).

As is consonant with other ecclesial statements more generally, the *Compendium*'s discussion of human rights displays a robustly deontological and personalist approach that grounds the possession of human rights in the inherent human dignity of the human person:

> The roots of human rights are to be found in the dignity that belongs to each human being. This dignity, inherent in human life and equal in every person, is perceived and understood first of all by reason. The natural foundation of rights appears all the more solid when, in light of the supernatural, it is considered that human dignity, after having been given by God and having been profoundly wounded by sin, was taken on and redeemed by Jesus Christ in his incarnation, death and resurrection. (*Compendium* 153)

In developing its discussion, the *Compendium* goes to indicate that these fundamental human rights are universal, inalienable, and inviolable, since they are "inherent in the human person and in human dignity" (*Compendium* 153). The value of dignity serves as the justificatory principle for attributing subjective rights to the human person, in that it serves to ground those rights. Within a Catholic conception of human rights, basic human rights are directed towards the flourishing or fulfillment of individuals-in-community, and accordingly, these basic rights both impose correlative duties and also imply associated responsibilities on the part of the rights bearer (the "subject" of the right).

The *Compendium* identifies the source of human dignity, which confers moral standing or moral considerability on the human person, with the human person's distinctive status as a creature created in the image of God. And in turn, the *Compendium* associates the image of God in humanity, first, with a cluster of various moral capacities, including moral subjectivity, self-knowledge or self-understanding, self-possession, moral freedom and self-determination, sociability, and relationality (i.e., the capacity to respond to another and to enter into relationship and communion). Second, the image of God is associated with various moral roles, including the responsibility to exercise dominion or stewardship over creation, and third, with a teleological ontology of interpersonal relationality. Finally, it is associated with the person's status as one possessing an ineliminable and unique vocation to communion with God and other human beings.

The *Compendium* concisely reiterates many of the claims that are discussed at significantly greater length in the International Theological Commission document, "Communion and Stewardship: Human Persons Created in the Image of God" (hereafter, *CS*). *CS* begins by affirming "that human persons are created in the Image of God in order to enjoy personal communion with the Father, Son and Holy Spirit and with one another in them, and in order to exercise, in God's name, responsible stewardship of the created world" (*CS* 4). It proceeds to elaborate this claim at considerable length, first by engaging the scriptural and traditional sources for this idea, and then second, by engaging the related ideas of interpersonal communion and ecological stewardship.

As is the case with the *Compendium*, the Commission characterizes the idea of the image of God in humanity in several ways: 1) in terms of the human person's fundamental orientation towards God, 2) in terms of the possession and exercise of immanent cognitive and affective capacities, 3) as an ontological (Trinitarian) structure of relation expressed actively in interpersonal relationships of love, 4) in its existential condition as undergoing an ongoing process of Christological restoration, and 5) in terms of moral or social functions of responsibility towards Creation and stewardship of it. In invoking the anthropological vision of *Gaudium et spes*, the Commission situates the interpretation of the image of God motif within the theological context of the mysteries of creation and of redemption, and while maintaining the intrinsic value of the creation of the human person in the divine image, it also affirms the Christological determination and Trinitarian structure of the image.

Indeed, it is for the sake of this Trinitarian communion that human persons are created in the divine image. It is precisely this radical likeness to the triune God that is the basis for the possibility of the communion of creaturely beings with the uncreated persons of the Blessed Trinity. Created in the image of God, human beings are by nature bodily and spiritual, men and women made for one another, persons oriented towards communion with God and with one another, wounded by sin and in need of salvation, and destined to be conformed to Christ, the perfect image of the Father, in the power of the Holy Spirit (*CS* 25).

Given that the activities entailed by interpersonal communion and responsible stewardship engage the bodily as well as the spiritual—intellectual and affective—realities of the human person, the human person can be said to image God in the unified totality of her body and soul. The affirmation of the imaging of God in the totality of the person as "ensouled body" or "embodied spirit" is intended to guard against any dualistic attempt to reduce the person to any single intellectual capacity or property, and to underscore the nature of the person as an interpersonal being created for communion with other human beings and God.

In articulating the understanding of the meaning and significance of the imago Dei, then, the ecclesial sources under consideration incorporate (at least) four analytically distinct strands of theological reflection within the Christian tradition concerning this idea: 1) substantive approaches which identify the imago Dei with the possession and exercise of distinctive rational and/or spiritual capacities, 2) functional approaches which identify the imago Dei with some function or responsibility vis-à-vis creation, 3) relational approaches which identify the imago Dei with being in a state of relation with God and other human beings, and 4) eschatological/vocational approaches which identify the imago Dei with an ongoing and dynamic process which is eschatologically fulfilled. While the central identifying characteristics of each of these approaches constitute an ineliminable aspect of the human imaging of God, the third and fourth aspects clearly function as architectonic and set the parameters for the expression of the other characteristics.[9]

This last point is clearly evident in assessing the question of the grounds of moral considerability, the basis for moral standing. I have already noted above that the tradition's perspective is that, in the case of human beings at least, moral considerability is regarded as co-extensive with species membership.[10] In other words, it is simply in virtue of being a member of the human species that one is rendered morally considerable. Accordingly, moral standing is not determined by considerations of personal achievement or social status (e.g., age, race, sex, gender, health and impairment, professional status, academic or intellectual accomplishment, religion, virtuousness, or capacities for moral agency or personal autonomy), but by one's "sheer" humanity. If this were not the case, and some other criterion were actually determinative, then the tradition could not consistently extend moral considerability to those human beings who, as "marginal cases," fail to meet the necessary threshold for active personhood according to an alternate set of criteria, but whom the tradition has generally regarded as moral persons carrying equal inherent dignity (e.g., prenatal members of the species and those who are severely cognitively impaired) and possessing equal moral status, "simply in virtue of being human."

For the purposes of the present discussion, the critical issue is that from the perspective of Catholic social thought—again, at least in the case of human beings—the possession and exercise of various cognitive and affective capacities typically associated with the exercise of

---

[9] On these various approaches, see David Clough, *On Animals* and J. Wentzel van Huyssteen, *Alone in the World? Human Uniqueness in Science and Theology* (Grand Rapids: Eerdmans, 2006).

[10] This is not to deny that there are contemporary attempts to significantly resource and re-envision the tradition in ways that attempt to overcome its anthropocentric disposition and to significantly expand the moral circle so as to account better for our relationships and obligations to non-human animals. For one significant such attempt, see Camosy, *For Love of Animals*, and "Other Animals as Persons?"

moral agency has not been regarded as a necessary criterion for recognizing moral standing or for attributing moral rights. Rather, human beings are regarded as possessing equal and inherent dignity, simply in virtue of their humanity, and as bearers of moral rights, simply in virtue of that status.[11] Particular human beings may not meet the threshold criteria for the exercise of moral agency, as we typically conceive of it, or be morally or personally autonomous in the relevant sense, but they are nevertheless to be considered moral persons, whose inherent dignity and rights derive from their status as creatures of God loved into being and called into communion with God, and who are thereby entitled to our moral respect and concern.[12] The Commission expresses this point concisely when it locates moral standing in moral personality rather than in moral agency and argues that "the imago Dei consists in [the human person's] *fundamental orientation to God*, which is the basis of human dignity and of the inalienable rights of the human person" (*CS* 22).

If this characterization of the Catholic social tradition is a persuasive one, and it is conceded that from the traditional perspective, moral personality forms the basis for moral standing and the ascription of moral rights, then where does the concept of moral patiency enter into the discussion? After all, the tradition does not employ the categories of moral patiency and moral agency in developing its account of the moral basis of human rights; hence, the implication of their use, here, might be thought to signal the introduction of alien categories onto an existing theological framework. In response to this concern, one might argue that although the tradition does not explicitly employ the language of moral patiency, as bearers of inherent dignity, human persons are nevertheless to be effectively regarded as moral patients because

---

[11] Within the framework of Catholic social thought, "humanity" denotes a theological rather than merely biological category, but not in such a way as to drive a wedge between the two, as though a person's humanity were somehow separable from her/his biology.

[12] The tradition of Catholic social thought appears to adopt what the philosopher Mary Anne Warren has characterized as a "minimalist" definition of personhood, minimalist in the sense that it does not make moral agency a necessary condition for being a person or for full moral standing (for otherwise, how could the tradition consistently claim that embryos and fetuses and the severely cognitively impaired or demented—members of the species who have never exercised moral agency, or who no longer do—are nevertheless to be regarded as possessing full and equal moral standing and as full moral persons?). This characterization is bound to sound paradoxical, given that most would consider a theological or metaphysical conception of moral personhood to be anything other than "minimalist" (in the sense in which Anglo-American political philosophers tend to employ the term)—and for good reason. Yet the point of Warren's contrast between maximalist and minimalist conceptions of moral personhood is to push back against the (Kantian) assumption that moral agency (understood in terms of moral deliberation, choice, and moral autonomy) is a necessary condition for moral standing and for recognition as a moral person. See Warren, *Moral Status: Obligations to Persons and to Other Living Things*, 90-121.

they are recognized as legitimate "objects" of moral respect and concern and the beneficiaries of various moral duties and obligations on the part of moral agents. From our brief survey, it is clear that the tradition of Catholic social thought attributes rights to human beings in virtue of their status as moral persons—creatures who are to be valued for their own sakes and respected as ends in themselves and bearers of an inviolable dignity and a vocation to communion with God and other human persons. Yet, it is equally clear that in conceiving of the relationship between personhood and rights in the way that it does, the tradition rejects the claim that moral standing is contingent on the possession and/or exercise of any cognitive or affective capacity that is typically associated with the exercise of moral agency.[13] Even though the tradition conceives of moral personhood as the basis for the ascription of moral rights to human beings, it does so in a way that recognizes, and indeed, even emphasizes the patient-dimensions of moral personality.

That the tradition conceives of the relationship between moral personality and the possession of moral rights as it does sheds important light on how the tradition conceives of the idea of rights itself. For to assert that a being enjoys the status of moral patient is simply to assert that that the being is morally considerable, that the being matters morally, has moral standing, and so forth, and not necessarily to affirm that being's status as rights bearer. In living the moral life, we may recognize that we possess various obligations or duties to different creatures (and perhaps different kinds of creatures) without ascribing moral rights to those same creatures. There is, to put it succinctly, a normative gap between the recognition of the inherent/intrinsic value or moral standing of a creature and the affirmation that the creature is the subject of moral rights. One obvious candidate for bridging the gap

---

[13] Ecclesial documents go to some lengths in discussing the various moral rights of the human person that are to be recognized and protected by social institutions and governments, and there is significant overlap between ecclesial enumerations and those contained within the International Bill of Human Rights. The theological tradition goes beyond international law in articulating the basis or foundation for human dignity (the imago Dei), a foundation that is, from the perspective of international law, highly controversial. But in spite of this, the particular rights attributed to persons do not vary significantly. For a non-religious philosophical discussion of the moral foundations of human rights within the context of international law, see Michael Ignatieff, *Human Rights as Politics and as Idolatry* (Princeton: Princeton University Press, 2003), and for discussion from the perspective of a Christian legal philosopher, see Jeremy Waldron, *Dignity, Rank, and Rights* (Oxford: Oxford University Press, 2012) and "The Image of God: Rights, Reason, and Order" in *Christianity and Human Rights: An Introduction*, ed. John Witte and Frank Alexander (Cambridge: Cambridge University Press, 2010). For discussion of the participatory character of rights within Catholic social thought, see Meghan Clark, *The Vision of Catholic Social Thought: The Virtue of Solidarity and the Praxis of Human Rights* (Minneapolis: Fortress, 2014).

is the property of moral agency, such that persons are morally recognized in virtue of their moral personality (understood in terms of capacities associated with the exercise of moral agency or personal autonomy), and that the ascription of rights is premised on protecting and promoting moral agency (i.e., moral deliberation and choice). This is the central insight of what has been characterized as the "choice theory of rights." Crudely characterized, the choice theory holds that rights refer to powers on the behalf of the rights holder to control the duties of another. On the choice theory, rights can properly be regarded as offering protection that is conducive to the exercise of choice—the autonomy and self-determination of the rights holder. Rights effectively provide the rights holder with a type of moral sovereignty within the scope of the duties that affect her. Thus, H.L.A. Hart, the leading contemporary defender of the choice theory, describes rights as fulfilling the need for a protective perimeter of obligations surrounding the activity of the rights bearer in order to provide a protective sphere of personal choice.[14] On this view, the possession and exercise of capacities typically associated with moral agency (consciousness, moral reflection and deliberation, autonomous self-direction) would be sufficient for the ascription of rights.

While this option may be an attractive one for a variety of reasons, it cannot be the view implicit in the ecclesial statements that we have canvassed, for as we have seen, the Catholic social tradition admits to the community of rights particular human beings who have not/never, or who no longer, display the capacities associated with developed moral agency. Within the moral logic of the tradition (at least in its contemporary expression), the exercise of moral agency or of personal autonomy has not been a prerequisite for rights ascription.

If, from the traditional perspective, moral agency cannot properly be regarded as the normative bridge, does another candidate present itself? If rights are regarded not as directly protecting spheres of moral choice but rather as protecting certain essential interests (interests whose satisfaction are essential to the promotion of well-being or flourishing), then the effective criterion for rights ascription will be the latter, and if it can be shown that moral patients are indeed interest bearers in the sense described, then it may be legitimate to recognize them as rights bearers, on the basis of interest bearing. This is the key insight of what has been variously characterized as the "benefit theory of rights," which holds that the ascription of rights is justified in virtue of protecting and promoting the interests or well-being of the rights holder. On the interest theory, rights are relational in the sense that they imply obligations that are owed to someone, in that the duty or obligation implied by the right is an obligation to the rights holder

[14] H.L.A. Hart, "Legal Rights" in H.L.A. Hart, *Essays on Bentham: Jurisprudence and Political Theory* (Oxford: Clarendon, 1982), 162-93.

whose interest is protected by that right.[15] Hence, on the interest theory, in order to ascribe rights to a particular being it is necessary that the being possess essential interests and that it be capable of flourishing or failing to flourish.

While perhaps not perfectly coincident, the benefit theory is more amenable to the Catholic social tradition's perspective on rights ascription on those issues that are most critical. The traditional perspective conceives of all human persons as possessing essential interests and as being capable of flourishing or failing to flourish—even if it ultimately conceives of comprehensive human flourishing in non-reductionist (i.e., non-naturalistic) terms—and these essential interests (which are biological, psychological, but also spiritual) ground the attribution of particular rights (related to physical, psychological, and spiritual integrity and well-being), which serve to protect and to promote such interests. Conceiving of moral rights in this way helps to account for the moral inclusivity of the theological tradition concerning those human beings—marginal cases—whose various psychological or moral capabilities might not rise to the level needed in order to satisfy alternative standards of moral considerability required for rights ascription.[16] The adoption and employment of a benefit theory of rights opens up the possibility for a theological re-consideration of ascribing rights to non-human animals, and it is to this issue that I now turn.

From Human to Non-Human Animals: Moral Patients and Moral Status

The preceding discussion has focused on the issue of rights ascription in the case of human beings. Its main purpose was to unpack and to elucidate what is theoretically and practically at stake with the Catholic social tradition's conceptualization of moral rights, and how this conceptualization relates to issues of human dignity and moral agency. In this section and the section that follows, I intend to consider in further depth the question of the purported link between non-human animal moral agency and non-human animal rights, exploring issues of moral patiency and moral subjectivity respectively. Previously, I noted two critical observations concerning the Catholic theological tradition's conceptions of the human person and our relationship to non-human animals.

---

[15] See works by Joseph Raz: "Hart on Moral Rights and Legal Duties," Oxford *Journal of Legal Studies* Vol. 4, no. 1 (Spring 1984): 123-31, "On the Nature of Rights," *Mind* Vol. 93, no. 370 (April 1984): 194-214, "Liberating Duties," *Law and Philosophy* Vol. 8, no. 1 (1989): 3-21, and "Duties of Well-Being" and "Rights and Individual Well-Being," in *Ethics and the Public Domain* (New York: Oxford University Press, 1995), 3-28 and 44-59.

[16] See Robert Garner, *A Theory of Justice for Animals* (New York: Oxford University Press, 2013).

First, the possession and exhibition of moral agency—in the sense of moral reflection, deliberation, and choice—has not generally been regarded as a necessary condition of moral considerability. The tradition has affirmed the equal intrinsic value or equal inherent dignity of the human person from the moment of conception through to natural death, regardless of potential or actual levels of cognitive or affective functioning, and thereby is fully inclusive of all members of the human species in the moral community. This affirmation of the equal inherent dignity of every person effectively translates into an intra-species moral egalitarianism in the case of human beings, so that as moral persons and bearers of equal inherent value, human beings are subject to the same basic normative requirements of equal respect and concern.

Second, the tradition remains predominantly "anthropocentric" in orientation, at least in the qualified sense that it affirms the ongoing ontological and moral differentiation of human and non-human animals, and it subordinates the interests of non-human animals to those of humans. Even though human beings exist in a role of stewardship (rather than absolute proprietary right) in relation to the rest of creation (including non-human animals) and enjoy a relationship of kinship with non-human animals who are similarly caught up in the mysteries of creation and redemption, there is nevertheless not a flat ontological or moral plane between the human species and other animal species (*CS* 80). Accordingly, although the tradition may proscribe the infliction of needless suffering, and insist on the just treatment of animals, there is no existing traditionally-grounded moral prohibition on the "humane" use of animals (e.g., raising and eating animals, keeping animals as pets, keeping animals in zoos, scientific experimentation on animals), as long as such use is in accordance with principled limits.[17] Within (and perhaps as a consequence of) its anthropocentric orientation, the tradition considers non-human animals as moral patients—possessing some limited moral value and as such worthy of

---

[17] While increasingly sensitive to the welfare of animals through its adoption of a modified animal welfarist perspective—which seeks to reduce and to minimize the discernible suffering of non-human animals—the theological tradition has nevertheless stopped short of adopting a more radical animal rights perspective—which would entail the rejection of the claim that non-human animals are fitting "objects" of human use. Hence, although the tradition has affirmed (albeit in a very qualified and relatively limited way) the intrinsic value of non-human animal species, in failing to challenge the dominant Western cultural view of non-human animals as property rather than as moral persons—for in the theological tradition's view, animals remain the property of God on loan to humanity—it remains committed to a species inegalitarianism that leaves open the theoretical and practical possibility of reducing animals to a merely instrumental value. The tradition's commitment to animal welfarism rather than to a more robust animal rights view is due to its residual speciesism, the ontological and moral differentiation of human and non-human animals. On the distinction between animal welfare and animal rights approaches, see Francione, *Animals, Property, and the Law* and *Animals as Persons*.

respect and concern—but not as moral persons—possessing the same inherent or intrinsic value as human beings.[18] By conceiving of non-human animals as moral patients but not as moral persons the tradition allows for the possibility of direct moral duties or obligations to non-human animals on the part of human beings (such as the obligation not to inflict disproportionate suffering), but it falls short of ascribing rights to non-human animals.[19]

Nonetheless, in spite of these factors, I want to suggest that the moral logic of the tradition does not preclude the possibility of attributing rights to animals, both as moral patients, and as I shall explain in the next section, as moral subjects.[20]

If the tradition of Catholic social thought recognizes the inherent dignity or intrinsic value of non-human animals (in virtue of being God's creatures) and also acknowledges that some particular animal species are both conscious (to varying degrees) and interest bearing, and simultaneously maintains that human beings have direct duties to animals in virtue of the moral reality of their creatureliness, then the *a priori* blanket exclusion of non-human animals from consideration as

---

[18] That animals are considered to be moral patients is clear from the various recent ecclesial statements that prescribe the just treatment of animals. Non-human animals are characterized theologically as God's creatures, as "divine gift" (along with the rest of creation), and as partners with humanity in the redemptive and eschatologically directed process of "cosmic communion." Moreover, in its discussion of the human practices that fall within the scope of the "responsible use" of non-human animals, the normative criterion that the tradition employs relates to the dignity of non-human animals as well as their capacities for suffering and for flourishing. Hence, animals are recognized as possessing dignity and value, as part of the dignity and goodness of divine creation, and as "creatures" rather than mere "objects" or "things." The tradition appears to recognize that as beings possessing varying degrees of consciousness, these non-human animal species also carry with them various moral interests (e.g., in avoiding pain, in sociality, in persisting in being). For discussion of these points, see Camosy, *Peter Singer and Christian Ethics*, 83-136, and "Intellectual Strangers No More? Peter Singer and Roman Catholicism on Ecological Concern," *Claritas* Vol. 1, no. 2 (Oct 2012); and John Berkman and Stanley Hauerwas, "The Chief End of All Flesh," *Theology Today* Vol. 49, no. 2 (July 1992).

[19] On the distinction of direct versus indirect duties to animals, see Regan, *Defending Animal Rights*, 39-65.

[20] A potential case for rights ascription could also be made on the basis of the analogous moral agency of at least some non-human animals, but this case is much more tentative, given the current contestation surrounding questions of animal agency. For further discussion of this issue, see for example, Jean Porter, "Nature, Normative Grammars, and Moral Judgments" in *Evolution, Games, and God* ed. Sarah Coakley and Martin Nowak (Cambridge, MA: Harvard University Press, 2013), 289-306, Porter, "The Natural Law and the Normative Significance of Nature," *Studies in Christian Ethics* Vol. 26, no. 2 (May 2013), 166-73. Also see Celia Deane Drummond, "Are Animals Moral? Taking Soundings through Vice, Virtue, Conscience, and the Imago Dei," in *Creaturely Theology*, ed. Celia Deane Drummond and David Clough (London: SCM Press, 2009), 190-210 and "In God's Image and Likeness in Humans and Other Animals: Performative Soul-Making and Graced Nature," *Zygon* Vol. 47, no. 4 (2012), 934-48.

potential moral rights bearers on the basis of species membership can only appear arbitrary. If, as living creatures, non-human animals express the goodness of divine creation in a distinctive way (or in distinctive ways, for there is no reason to assume axiological monism), and for this reason, are conceived either of being intrinsically valuable—valuable in themselves, aside from any benefit they provide to other creatures—or of possessing dignity (as creatures), then this provides a *prima facie* reason for recognizing their status as moral patients, and an initial (though perhaps not sufficient) consideration for ascribing to them moral rights.

But, moreover, if (as on the interest theory of rights) rights serve primarily to protect and to promote various essential interests that are conducive to the well-being or flourishing of the creature, then, if non-human animal creatures can be said to possess such interests (e.g., in avoiding pain, in persisting in being, in being free) there appears to be little reason not to extend by way of analogy the concept of moral rights to (interest bearing) non-human animals on the basis of their status as moral patients.[21] Just as (on the tradition's account) all human beings are considered to be interest bearing and subject to flourish (or to fail to flourish), so too are/do various animals, whose status as

[21] To some, the ascription of moral rights based on considerations of moral patiency will seem overly expansive, in that it may appear to display a lack of discrimination concerning the reality of ontological and moral differentiation amongst different kinds of creatures, who exhibit varying in degrees of complexity, and to allow for the possibility of counter-intuitively attributing rights to creatures whom we would not imagine to be rights bearers (e.g., plants or slugs). Yet, as I have suggested, moral patiency in itself may not be sufficient for rights ascription. In the case of non-human animals, "mere creatureliness" may be sufficient to confer moral standing on a creature so as to render the creature a moral patient, but insufficient to justify the ascription of rights to the creature, save in a very general sense of "a legitimate entitlement (right) to moral respect." In so far as they specify norms of treatment of creatures, rights conceived as deontological constraints set limits on human action and can generate direct moral duties or obligations. Hence, it can be argued that all creatures possess a basic right to respect, which entails that they should be treated in such a way as to respect the moral reality of their creatureliness (even if the concrete content of the principle—what the principle of respect requires—remains somewhat indeterminate). However, what is required for the ascription of rights in a more determinate sense is either the possession of essential interests connected to well-being, or the possession of capacities typically associated with the exercise of moral agency, or some third alternative. If one foregoes the moral agency option, then one is presented with the case of interest bearing moral patients. On the interest theory of rights, there is an essential connection between interests and well-being such that a being qualifies as interest bearing if it can flourish (or fail to flourish) in accordance with the kind of creature that it is. Given the ontological differentiation of various living creatures, some essential interests will be shared across kinds of creatures, and others will be distinctive, and different interests (e.g., an interest in avoiding pain, or in continuing to exist, or in being free to act) will justify the ascription of different rights. For a general discussion of these issues, see Alasdair Cochrane's benefit theory of animal rights in Cochrane, *Animal Rights without Liberation*.

moral patients should qualify them as rights bearing entities. The only reason for withholding such recognition in the case of non-human animals appears to be an ontological and moral privileging of humans over non-human animals.[22]

There are good reasons, then, given the moral logic implicit in the Catholic social tradition's treatment of the moral rights of human beings, for maintaining the possibility of rights ascription in the case of some non-human animals on the basis of their status as moral patients.[23] In the next section, I discuss a different line of argument that might be offered in support of animal rights—one that argues for the ascription of moral rights to animals on the basis of their moral subjectivity. As I will explain, the argument from animal moral subjectivity, while bearing important similarities to the argument from animal moral agency, involves the defense of claims that are less ambitious conceptually and empirically, and thus, easier and less controversial to sustain than are claims involving right ascription on the basis of animal moral agency.

MORAL PERSONALITY: MORAL PATIENTS, MORAL AGENTS, AND MORAL SUBJECTS

In discussing the Catholic social tradition's views concerning the foundations of moral rights, I noted that the tradition's overall concep-

---

[22] As David Clough has recently suggested, the biblical theological data makes it very difficult to deny both these two claims: 1) that there are extensive ontological (and correlative moral) differences amongst animal species/animal creatures and 2) that human beings are nevertheless morally distinctive in the order of creation. See Clough, *On Animals*, and also Camosy, "Other Animals as Persons?" Once one admits the extent of the reality of ontological and moral differentiation, the challenge is to avoid reinstating some form of hierarchicalism in ethical practice, so that when there are conflicts of interests between human and non-human animals, the interests of human animals automatically or inevitably trump those of non-human animals. Ontological and moral differentiation appears to apply pressure against any practical form of species egalitarianism. For more on this, see Francione, *Animals as Persons* and "Animal Welfare and the Moral Value of Nonhuman Animals," *Law, Culture, and the Humanities* Vol. 6, no. 1 (2010).

[23] In "Other Animals as Persons?" Charles Camosy argues for the broadening of our understandings of morality and of moral personality in order to expand the moral circle and to include at least some non-human animals as moral persons. Although Camosy is concerned to establish the moral standing of non-human animals and not to ascribe moral rights to non-human animals on the basis of their moral standing as persons, an analysis of the kind that he advances might be employed to do so. One considerable challenge that the attempt at such an expansion faces is that of addressing adequately the highly contested status of the concept of moral personhood. For more on this issue, in addition to Warren, *Moral Status*, see also David DeGrazia, "Great Apes, Dolphins, and the Concept of Personhood," *Southern Journal of Philosophy* Vol. 35 (1997), 310-20. See also Christopher Morris, "The Idea of Moral Standing," Sarah Chan and John Harris, "Human Animals and Nonhuman Persons," and Michael Tooley, "Are Nonhuman Animals Persons?," in *The Oxford Handbook of Animal Ethics*, ed. Tom Beauchamp and R.G. Frey (New York: Oxford University Press, 2011).

tualization of the image of God motif incorporates substantive moral capacities in addition to functional, relational, and eschatological properties. Up to this point, the ensuing discussion has focused on the issue of the attribution of moral rights to human and non-human animals on the basis of their moral status as moral patients. At one level, what grounds this status of moral patiency, I have suggested, is the recognition of the basic inviolability—inherent dignity or intrinsic value—of human and non-human animal creatures. Divine activity in creating and sustaining these creatures in being confers moral value on them in virtue of their created goodness, and entitles them to moral respect. At the same time, and at another level, these creatures are properly considered "objects" of moral concern in virtue of their possessing essential interests and the capacity to flourish. Both of these properties serve together to ground the ascription of various moral rights (which are correlated to the protection and promotion of physical, psychological, and spiritual flourishing or well-being) to these creatures, and thus, constitute one reason for asserting the theological intelligibility of the moral rights of non-human animals.

In addition to considering moral rights under the aspect of moral patiency, however, one might also consider it under the aspect of moral agency (correlated more closely to the substantive, functional, and relational capacities described above). Empirical studies do appear to confirm that different animals do in fact exhibit signs of consciousness, of emotion, and of purposive behavior, and in some cases, of language, and thus suggest that this may be a promising avenue for theological and ethical reflection.[24] An account of animal rights focused on considerations of moral agency would depart from the account of moral rights outlined in the previous section of this essay, which I have suggested is based primarily on considerations of moral personality understood in terms of moral patiency. To shift focus from an account centered on considerations of moral patiency to one centered on considerations of moral agency would appear to necessitate one of two options. 1) Either there is appeal to an account of the moral status of exceptional cases (marginal cases) who do not fit neatly into established categories of developed moral agency that are required for rights ascription, but that we (intuitively?) recognize ought to be accorded rights. 2) Or, there is a call for a significant revision of our dominant understandings of moral agency that those "on the margins" might be included within the moral community and thereby recognized as full rights bearing members of it.

---

[24] See Donald Griffin, *Animal Minds: Beyond Cognition to Consciousness* (Chicago: University of Chicago Press, 2001); Frans DeWaal, *Good Natured: The Origins of Right and Wrong in Humans and Other Animals* (Cambridge, MA: Harvard University Press, 1997); and Marc Bekoff, *Wild Justice: The Moral Lives of Animals* (Chicago: University of Chicago Press, 2009).

The difficulty the first option is that it will be inconsistent, *ad hoc*, and piecemeal. The difficulty with the second is that even in the intra-specific case of human beings alone, the identification of any particular substantive capability that is sufficiently broad enough in scope will likely prove elusive at best, and morally exclusive at worst, a fact that is only compounded with the widening of the moral circle to include all human and non-human animals.[25] Aside from this challenge of identifying a set of morally relevant capacities shared by both human and non-human animals, however, the ongoing philosophical and scientific discussion concerning the mental life and moral agency of animals remains a complex and highly contested one, and for this reason, it might (at least at present) constitute a fragile basis on which to construct a sustainable theory of the rights of non-human animals.[26]

If the present prospects for developing a theory of non-human animal rights based on an account of animal moral agency appear unpromising, we may mistakenly infer that we are limited to developing one based on considerations of moral patiency. However, advocates of animal rights have begun to develop a third type of account, a hybrid theory that selectively incorporates agent and patient-dimensions under the concept of moral subjectivity. Although this account has roots in the theory of animal rights developed by Tom Regan and his early work, the *Case for Animal Rights*, it has undergone significant transformation and revision in response to criticisms of Regan's theory.[27]

The core concept in Regan's theory of animal rights is that of a "subject of a life" by which Regan means those beings that are conscious and that possess beliefs, desires, perceptions, memories, a sense of the future, a subjective sense of one's interests, and an ability to initiate action. This list includes some qualities that we might associate with capacities related to the exercise of moral agency (the ability to deliberate concerning possible courses of action and then to initiate). It is an extensive list and appears to include certain non-human animals and to exclude many others. As such, it has been subject to extensive critique.[28] For Regan, the basic animal right is the right to respect, which precludes an entity being treated as a mere means, whose

---

[25] For more on this point, see Nicholas Wolsterstorff's critique of capacity based approaches to moral considerability in Wolsterstorff, *Justice: Rights and Wrongs* (Princeton: Princeton University Press, 2008).

[26] This is part of the argument made by Marian Stamp Dawkins in *Why Animals Matter*, where Dawkins argues for restraint in developing moral claims based on animal consciousness. See also Gary Steiner's argument in *Animals and the Moral Community* and that of Gary Francione in "Taking Sentience Seriously," in Francione, *Animals as Persons*, 129-47.

[27] Regan, *The Case for Animal Rights*. See also Regan, *Defending Animal Rights* and *Animal Rights, Human Wrongs* (Lanham: Rowman and Littlefield, 2003).

[28] For example, see Francione, *Rain without Thunder*; Steiner, *Animals and the Moral Community*; Warren, "Difficulties with the Strong Animal Rights Position," and also,

interests and well-being are rendered subject to a utilitarian calculus. Hence, on Regan's view, rights protect essential interests and function primarily as *prima facie* trumps that may override other moral considerations based on utility.

Recent advocates of deontological accounts of animal rights, such as Gary Francione, and Will Kymlicka and Sue Donaldson, have adopted and modified aspects of Regan's account while maintaining the core insights of the theory.[29] In his work on animal rights, Francione has consistently argued for the consideration of non-human animals as moral persons, whose moral interests and well-being merit respect and concern. While acknowledging the scientific data concerning the presence of higher order mental capacities in many animal species, Francione's argument focuses primarily on the issue of sentience, and on how sentience gives rise to moral standing on the part of its bearer. Francione's overall argument for animal rights pairs the deontological emphases of Regan's account with the concern for experiential well-being addressed by utilitarian accounts such as that of Peter Singer. What drives Francione's argument is the intuitive conviction, grounded in lived experience that (at least some) non-human animals simply are moral persons, and that as persons, they ought to be treated as ends-in-themselves and as bearers of an inviolable dignity, not subject to ownership, use, or exploitation by human beings.[30]

The concern for the inter-relation between the capacity for experiential well-being, and moral standing is also exhibited in the account of group differentiated animal citizenship developed by Will Kymlicka and Sue Donaldson. In a way that echoes Francione's account, Kymlicka and Donaldson appeal to the first person intuitive experience of animal subjectivity as the main evidence of the reality of the

---

Rowlands, *Animal Rights: Moral Theory and Practice*. Ironically, the bulk of criticism of Regan's account has focused not on his characterization of the various capacities possessed by a subject of a life, but on his adoption of the idea of intrinsic value, which has been repeatedly rejected by critics as "mysterious" and "ephemeral." In an earlier formulation of his theological defense of animal rights, Andrew Linzey adopts something very close to Regan's conception of the subject of a life, and Linzey's account has been subject to a similar criticism (that the moral circle implied by the subject of a life criterion is actually fairly narrow, and includes only a very small number of non-human animal species). See Linzey, *Christianity and the Rights of Animals*, and *Animal Theology*.

[29] Gary Francione, *Rain without Thunder* and *Animals as Persons* and Will Kymlicka and Sue Donaldson, *Zoopolis: A Political Theory of Animal Rights* (New York: Oxford University Press, 2011).

[30] For Francione, the most compelling piece of evidence in support of the moral personality of non-human animals is not the most recent empirical data on animal consciousness, but rather, our first-personal lived experience of the moral subjectivity of non-human animals. Francione argues that the reality of the moral personality of non-human animals is first confirmed through our lived encounter with them, and through that experience we become better aware of what conduces to the flourishing of these creatures.

moral personality (or, as they express it, "selfhood") of non-human animals. On Kymlicka and Donaldson's account, rights—which again are conceived as instruments that serve to protect and to promote the conditions that are required for flourishing—are the just entitlements of all conscious and sentient human and non-human animals. According to Kymlicka and Donaldson:

> Conscious/sentient beings are selves—that is, they have a distinctive subjective experience of their own lives and of the world.... Sentience/consciousness has a distinct moral significance because it enables a subjective experience of the world.... Beings who experience their lives from the inside, and for whom life can go better and worse are selves, not things, whom we recognize as experiencing vulnerability—to pleasure and pain, to frustration and satisfaction, to joy and suffering, or to fear and death.[31]

What the animal rights theories of Francione and of Kymlicka and Donaldson share in common is the conviction that the capacity for experiential well-being (which presupposes some level of consciousness) can form the basis for moral standing, and in turn, the attribution of moral rights. If Francione and Kymlicka and Donaldson are correct in arguing that our concrete lived experience of non-human animals can generate an intuitive recognition of the inherent value of animals as moral subjects who possess essential interests that are related to their flourishing or well-being, then the phenomenon of moral subjectivity or selfhood may indeed be sufficient (though as we have seen, not necessary) to justify the ascription of rights to non-human animals, and to thereby provide a second and complementary foundation for affirming the rights of both human and non-human animals.[32]

---

[31] Kymlicka and Donaldson, *Zoopolis*, 24-5. As is the case with Francione, for Kymlicka and Donaldson, confirmation of the moral personality of non-human animals comes through our concrete experience of non-human animals as moral subjects or selves rather than through scientific data or empirical confirmation. On both of these accounts, the moral subjectivity of non-human animals is something that is experienced immediately within the context of moral experience.

[32] Grounding moral rights in considerations of moral subjectivity in no way excludes the possibility of an overlapping and more fundamental grounding in considerations of moral patiency. Rather, the concurrent recognition of human and non-human animals as both moral patients and as moral subjects exemplifies a pluralistic and multilayered approach to the ascription of moral rights. But why should we require, or even allow for a complementary justification? Given that rights can be seen to be justified in terms of various essential interests, and that essential interests are to at least some extent fluid across species, in that there may be some essential interests that fall across some or many animal species (e.g., the interest to avoid suffering), and other interests that are specific to only some animal species (e.g., the interest in moral self-direction), formulating rights on the basis of variant interests will allow for the development of a group differentiated conception of animal rights, which recognizes varying obligations or duties to different animal species. Hence, instead of being compelled to recognize a single criterion for moral status (e.g. consciousness, sentience, rationality),

The relational character of these accounts of moral rights as grounded in considerations of moral subjectivity is consonant with the theological tradition's affirmation of moral personality as encompassing not only fundamental moral capacities in a process of ongoing development and transformation, but also the fundamental relationality of the human person that is made manifest both in kinship with God, other human persons, and non-human creatures, and also in the manifestation of the divine image in the continuing exercise of responsible stewardship in relation to the other members of divine creation.

Conclusion

Moving by way of analogy from human to non-human animals, in this article, I have sought to defend the claim that the ascription of moral rights to non-human animals in virtue of their moral standing both as moral patients and as moral subjects is consonant with the moral logic of the Catholic social tradition. Although the tradition has generally been reticent about the possibility of attributing moral rights to non-human animals, there are nevertheless existing resources within it for affirming the theological coherence of non-human animals as moral rights bearers. As our knowledge and experience of human and non-human animal species continues to expand, so too may the potential for developing a case for ascribing moral rights to non-human animals on the basis of moral agency. At present, however, the recognition of non-human animals both as moral patients and as moral subjects is fit to the task. M

---

in view of the ontological diversity of creatures, we can allow for the possibility that different properties may effectively generate varying grounds of moral standing for different creatures, and so serve as different justificatory principles for the ascription of moral rights. For more on this, see Warren, *Moral Status*, DeGrazia, "Moral Status as a Matter of Degree?" and Cochrane, *Animal Rights without Liberation*.

CONTRIBUTORS

John Berkman is Associate Professor of Moral Theology at Regis College, University of Toronto. He is the author of many articles on the moral significance of non-human animals for Christian theology and ethics. He also publishes in the areas of biomedical ethics, Thomistic moral theology, and social justice, including *Searching for a Universal Ethic: Multidisciplinary, Ecumenical and Inter-faith Responses to the Catholic Natural Law Tradition*, edited with William C. Mattison III (Eerdmans, 2015), *The Pinckaers Reader*, edited with Craig Titus, (CUA Press, 2005), and *The Hauerwas Reader*, edited with Michael Cartwright (Duke University Press, 2001).

Charles C. Camosy is Associate Professor of Theology at Fordham University. He is the author of *Peter Singer and Christian Ethics: Beyond Polarization* (Cambridge University Press, 2012), *Too Expensive to Treat?—Finitude, Tragedy, and the Neonatal ICU* (Eerdmans, 2010), and *For Love of Animals: Christian Ethics, Consistent Action* (Franciscan, 2013). His latest book, *Abortion: Beyond Polarization and a Way Forward*, is forthcoming from Eerdmans in March of 2015.

Celia Deane-Drummond is Professor of Theology at the University of Notre Dame. She holds Ph.Ds. in plant physiology and theology. Her more recent books include *Wonder and Wisdom: Conversations in Science, Spirituality and Theology* (DLT, 2006), *Genetics and Christian Ethics* (Cambridge University, 2006), *Ecotheology* (DLT, 2008), *Christ and Evolution: Wonder and Wisdom* (Fortress/SCM Press, 2009), *Creaturely Theology: On God, Humans and Other Animals*, edited with David Clough (SCM Press, 2009), *Seeds of Hope: Facing the Challenge of Climate Justice* (CAFOD, 2010), *Religion and Ecology in the Public Sphere*, edited with Heinrich Bedford-Strohm (Continuum, 2011), *Animals as Religious Subjects*, edited with Rebecca Artinian Kaiser and David Clough (Bloomsbury 2013), and *The Wisdom of the Liminal* (Eerdmans, 2014).

James Helmer is Assistant Professor of Christian Ethics at Xavier University. His main research interests lie in the areas of Christian social and political ethics, comparative religious ethics, biomedical ethics, and theology and science. He has published in The *Journal of the Society of Christian Ethics*, and *Studies in Christian Ethics*, and has completed a book manuscript in the area of religion, multiculturalism, and human rights.

Susan Kopp is Professor of Health Sciences and a veterinarian at LaGuardia Community College (City University of New York). A scholar at Yale Interdisciplinary Center for Bioethics, she chairs the Center's animal ethics study group and was a contributor to the Hastings Center special report: *Animal Research Ethics: Evolving Views and Practices (2012)*. Recipient of the Eileen Egan Award for outstanding journalism, she has also written for Focolare Movement's magazine, *Living City*.

Julie Hanlon Rubio is Professor of Christian Ethics at St. Louis University. Her research brings together Christian theology on marriage and family and Catholic social teaching. She is the author of *A Christian Theology of Marriage and Family* (Paulist Press, 2003) and *Family Ethics: Practices for Christians* (Georgetown University Press, 2010). Her new book, *Between the Personal and the Political: Catholic Hope for Common Ground,* will be published by George-town University Press in 2015.

Jean Porter is the John A. O'Brien Professor of Theological Ethics at the University of Notre Dame. She is the author of five books, including *Ministers of the Law: A Natural Law Theory of Legal Authority* (Eerdmans, 2010) and *Nature as Reason: A Thomistic Theory of the Natural Law* (Eerdmans, 2005), and numerous articles on historical and foundational moral theology, the moral thought of Aquinas, and related topics. She is currently working on a book on Aquinas' treatment of justice as a virtue.

JMT

JOURNAL • OF

M • O • R • A • L

THEOLOGY

Upcoming Issues

Technology
Volume 4, Number 1 (January 2015)
Editors: James F. Caccamo
and David Matzko McCarthy

Open to all Submissions
Volume 4, Number 2 (June 2015)
Editor: David Matzko McCarthy

Disability
Volume 5, Number 1 (January 2016)
Editor: Miguel J. Romero
and David Matzko McCarthy

Open to all Submissions
Volume 5, Number 2 (June 2016)
Editor: David Matzko McCarthy
and Jason King

***Populorum Progressio*: 50 Years**
Volume 6, Number 1 (January 2017)
Editor: Mari Rapela Heidt
and Matthew A. Shadle

Open to all Submissions
Volume 6, Number 2 (June 2017)
Editor: Jason King

Articles available to view or download at:

www.msmary.edu/jmt